Spotlight On

Prague

Written by Zoe Ross

Published by AA Publishing, a trading name of Automobile Association Developments Limited, whose registered office is Fanum House, Basing View, Basingstoke, Hampshire, RG21 4EA. Registered number 1878835.

Packaged for Automobile Association Developments Limited by IL&FS, New Delhi

A CIP catalogue record for this book is available from the British Library.

ISBN 978-0-7495-5476-7

Colour separation by KDP
Printed and bound in China by Leo Paper Products

A03233
Maps in this title produced from mapping © MAIRDUMONT / Falk Verlag 2007
Transport map © Communicarta Ltd, UK

CONTENTS

Staré Město

Hradčany

Josefov

Malá
Strana

Nové
Město

Further
Afield

Prague

It would have to be a very hardened traveller indeed who could arrive in Prague and not be instantly awed by the grandeur of the city. From the Vltava River, crossed by the spectacular Charles Bridge, one of the 15 bridges across the river, to the stunning façade of the castle high on its hill looking down over the city, and the breathtaking combination of Gothic, baroque and art nouveau architecture in the Old and New towns, this is a city that rivals most other great capitals of Europe.

Even though Stone Age remains have been found in the area, Prague's history can clearly be traced back to the 10th century when the Přemyslid tribe of Bohemia began their 500-year rule. By the Middle Ages it had become an important trading centre in this part of Europe, which gave rise to the Old Town. Later, it was the seat of residence for Charles IV, the Holy Roman Emperor, who turned the city into a revered centre of learning and culture in the 1400s. However, in the following century the Hussite Wars divided the country. The city became something of a backwater under Habsburg rule, although during the reign of

the great art lover Rudolf II, many artists, astrologers and scientists gathered here.

It wasn't until the late 17th century that the city once again saw a period of revival that contributed largely to Prague's present-day beauty. Catholicism once again became the religion of the Czech people and the fashion for baroque architecture that was spreading across Europe inspired beautiful and intricately decorated churches, notably the two churches of St Nicholas in the Old Town and Lower Quarter.

By the 19th century, the Czechs had grown tired of foreign rule and the National Revival period began launching

the Iron Curtain as part of Eastern Europe's Communist regime.

As the Cold War raged, it seemed that Prague's beauty and charm were lost to the outside world for good. However, in 1989 the people rose up in demonstrations and workers' strikes, encouraged and supported by playwright and political dissident Václav Havel, to protest against the repressive government under which they lived. The relative calm with which the downfall of the Communists came about earned it the epithet "Velvet Revolution".

Amost overnight the Czech Republic (Slovakia became independent in 1992) was back on the world stage and over the ensuing decade word spread about the wonders of its capital city and a tourism boom began that has not waned since.

Now protected by UNESCO as a World Heritage Site, the five areas of the city centre offer delights at every turn, be they architectural, historical, cultural or commercial. Furthermore, the abundance of lush green spaces in Prague gives it an advantage over other European cities. Petřin Park, Vyšehrad and Letná are all just minutes from the centre, but feel like another world, far from the ceaseless bustle along the cobbled streets.

Culture buffs are bound to be spoilt for choice in the city, with concerts, superb art galleries and museums, baroque palaces and striking churches on offer. By day Prague is a shopper's paradise, particularly for its world-renowned Bohemian glass; at night, the pace doesn't slacken at all with its large number of pubs, beer houses, clubs and atmospherically smoky jazz venues coming to life. It's little wonder that the city has become a favourite for stag and hen parties in recent years – night owls will be in their element here.

In short, the Czech capital has something for everyone: serene or sassy, verdant or vibrant, traditional or trendy, it's a city that justly deserves its nickname "Golden Prague".

a resurgence in national culture and architecture with a strong patriotic theme. Following the collapse of the Austro-Hungarian Empire in 1918, Prague became the capital of independent Czechoslovakia. This period was short-lived though, as Hitler occupied the city and the rest of the country from 1939 to 1945, with dreadful consequences. During that time, almost the entire Jewish community of Prague, long established in the Josefov area, was wiped out. Stalin's Red Army may have seemed like a saviour when it took over the city in 1945, but three years later Czechoslovakia was firmly locked behind

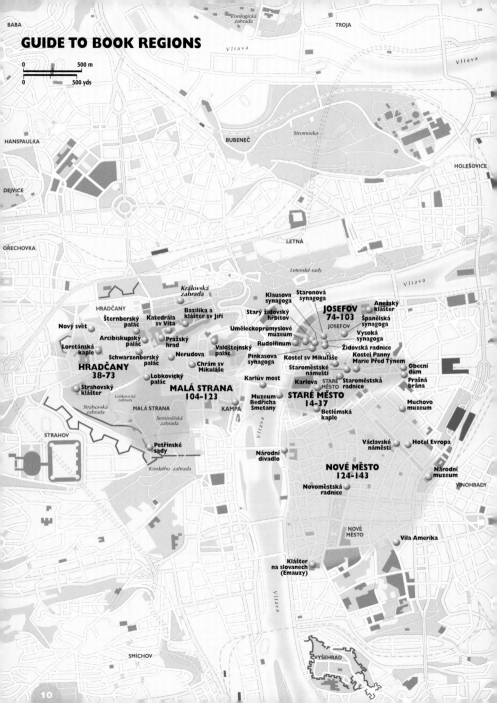

GUIDE TO BOOK REGIONS

0   500 m
0   500 yds

BABA

ZOOlogická zahrada

TROJA

Vltava

Vltava

HANSPAULKA

BUBENEČ

Stromovka

HOLEŠOVICE

DEJVICE

OŘECHOVKA

LETNÁ

Letenské sady

Vltava

HRADČANY
Nový svět

Šternberský palác

Arcibiskupský palác

Loretánská kaple

Schwarzenberský palác

**HRADČANY
38–73**

Strahovský klášter

STRAHOV

Strahovská zahrada

Královská zahrada

Katedrála sv Víta

Bazilika a klášter sv Jiří

Pražský hrad

Nerudova

Chrám sv Mikuláše

Lobkovický palác

Lobkovická zahrada

MALÁ STRANA

Seminářská zahrada

Petřínské sady

Kinského zahrada

Klausova synagoga

Staronová synagoga

Starý židovský hřbitov

Uměleckoprůmyslové muzeum

Rudolfinum

Valdštejnský palác

Pinkasova synagoga

Karlův most

Muzeum Bedřicha Smetany

KAMPA

Vltava

Národní divadlo

**JOSEFOV
74–103**

JOSEFOV

Anežský klášter

Španělská synagoga

Vysoká synagoga

Židovská radnice

Kostel Panny Marie Před Týnem

Kostel sv Mikuláše

Staroměstské náměstí

Karlova

STARÉ MĚSTO

Staroměstská radnice

Obecní dům

Prašná brána

Muchovo muzeum

**STARÉ MĚSTO
14–37**

Betlémská kaple

Václavské náměstí

Hotel Evropa

Národní muzeum

VINOHRADY

**NOVÉ MĚSTO
124–143**

Novoměstská radnice

NOVÉ MĚSTO

Vila Amerika

Klášter na slovanech (Emauzy)

Vltava

SMÍCHOV

VYŠEHRAD

**MALÁ STRANA
104–123**

10

Staré Město

No trip to the Czech capital should begin without a visit to the Old Town. Since the 11th century this has been the vibrant hub of the city and the layers of history that are the lifeblood of this fascinating area can be seen and felt in its streets, alleyways and architecture. The Old Town rose in importance as the home of the Bohemian royal family until they opted for the more strategic location of Hradčany in the 15th century, and many buildings, such as the protective gateways, still stand as reminders of those days. It was also the trading heart of the city, the core of which is still awash with commerce, though these days it largely caters to the multitude of tourists who come to admire its splendour.

STARÉ MĚSTO WALK

1. Staroměstské náměstí
See page 30

The Old Town Square is where most visitors strike out from. It is surrounded on all sides by spectacular buildings in a variety of architectural styles, from the Gothic to the baroque. At the centre of the square is the monument to the church reformer Jan Hus. Start your walk at the southeast corner of the square.

2. Kostel Panny Marie Před Týnem
See page 20

You can't miss the impressive steeples of this 14th-century church, which is probably the most important religious building in Prague. Look up at the pediment between the two steeples to see the gold statue of the Madonna gleaming down over the square. Cross the square to the northwest side.

3. Kostel sv Mikuláše
See page 22

The brilliant white façade of the Church of St Nicholas, topped by vibrant green domes, is one of Prague's most familiar sights, although the rather neglected interior is a disappointment. Nevertheless, the exterior is a baroque joy. Today the church is a popular venue for classical music concerts. Walk down to the southwest corner of the square.

4. Staroměstská radnice
See page 34

The vast Old Town Hall harmoniously blends Gothic and Renaissance styles, illustrating its original construction and subsequent renovations. Its most popular feature is the Astronomical Clock that draws large crowds every hour. Exit the square via the southeast corner and walk along Celetná to the junction with Uprasné brány.

5. Prašná brána
See page 28

The Powder Gate is a clear but beautiful reminder that the Old Town was once protected by gated entrances – some 13 in all – when the royal family resided here before moving to Hradčany. It is the most notable surviving gate in the city because of the incredibly intricate carvings on its façade.

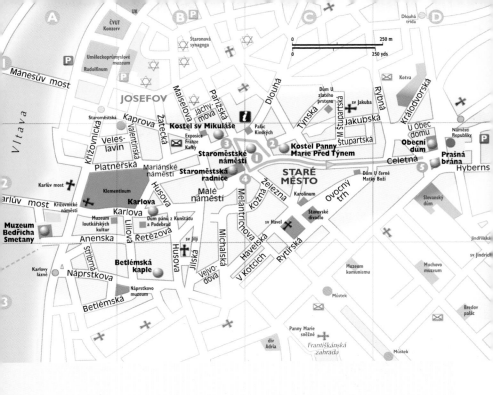

Betlémská kaple

In a city full of grand churches the Bethlehem Chapel is one of the most unassuming, but its history is intrinsic to Prague. Built in 1391, it was the chapel of choice for the great Czech hero Jan Hus, who preached his reformist sermons here between 1402 and 1413 before being imprisoned and burned at the stake.

✚ **17 B3**

✉ **Betlémská kaple**
  Betlémské náměstí

☎ 224 248 595

◷ Apr–Oct, Tue–Sun 10–6:30;
  Nov–Mar, Tue–Sun 10–5:30

✋ Inexpensive

Ⓜ Národní třída

By the 17th century the Jesuits had begun to exercise enormous power in the city and the chapel was given over to them in 1620. By 1786, however, it was little more than a ruin and was abandoned as a religious centre, eventually becoming a residential site. It was only in the 1950s, in honour of Hus and its history, that the city decided to rebuild the chapel to its original medieval design, closely following architectural sketches from the day.

Above: You can sit outside the tall, twin-gabled Bethlehem Chapel, for centuries the centre of the Reformation movement

Karlova

From the 15th to the 17th centuries the kings of Bohemia celebrated their coronations by parading through the city from the Old Town to the castle. Karlova (Charles Street), named after the 14th-century Holy Roman Emperor Charles IV, was one of the main streets on this route, leading to the Charles Bridge across the Vltava.

Despite its rather touristy feel you can still sense the historic importance in the many Gothic, Renaissance and baroque buildings that line Karlova. The most beautiful baroque house is at the Golden Well (U Zlaté studny) at No 3, with carved reliefs of religious figures on its façade. Further along at No 18 is the

House at the Golden Snake (U Zlatého hada), considered to be the oldest surviving café in the city, dating back to the early 18th century. At the far end of the street is the vast Klementinum complex, originally established by the Jesuits, then expanded into a university building. Today it is home to the National Library.

Above: Hotel U Zlaté studny (Golden Well), a 16th-century building on Karlova

✠ **17 B2**

✉ **Karlova**

Ⓜ Staroměstská

Kostel Panny Marie
Před Týnem

The Gothic 80m (262-foot) high spires of the Church of Our Lady before Týn (also known as the Týn Cathedral) are one of the most recognisable sights in Prague, looming over the landscape of the Old Town Square. Built in 1365, the church became the focus of attention between the 15th to the 17th centuries when the Hussites used it as a centre to launch their reformist church movement. This came to an end in 1620 when the so-called Battle of the White Mountain saw Protestant Bohemia defeated by Catholic Austria and the beginning of the Thirty Years War. The church's façade is its most prominent feature, and is particularly beautiful when floodlit at night, but inside there are many treasures to be seen, including an elaborate pulpit and medieval font, and a post-1620 statue of the Madonna.

The north entrance of the church is carved with scenes of Christ's Passion. There are also some baroque details, such as the altar, which were added in the 18th century after part of the church was burnt.

The church is the burial site of Tycho Brahe (1546–1601), the brilliant Danish astronomer, who spent his last years in Prague working in the court of Emperor Rudolf II with his assistant Johannes Kepler. Various mysteries surround Brahe's death; many historians believe he was murdered by the ambitious and subsequently influential Kepler, although it is far more likely that he inadvertently poisoned himself with the chemicals he used in his work.

Above left: The Gothic spires of Týn Church
Above right: Horse-drawn carriages are a reminder of the past

✠ **17 C2**

✉ **Kostel Panny Marie Před Týnem**
Staroměstské náměstí 604

☎ 222 318 186

🌐 **www.tynska.farnost.cz**

🕐 Services Tue, Fri 5pm, Wed–Thu 6pm, Sat 8am, Sun 9:30am and 9pm

✋ Free

Ⓜ Staroměstská

Kostel sv Mikuláše

Probably Prague's most beautiful church, the magnificent Church of St Nicholas (not to be confused with its namesake in the Malá Strana quarter) was constructed in 1735 by the great baroque architect Kilián Ignaz Dientzenhofer.

St Nicholas's makes for a wonderful entrance to the Old Town Square, its white towers and green domes resembling a fairy-tale palace. At the time of its construction for the Benedictine order, the church was surrounded by other residential buildings, since demolished. This explains why Dientzenhofer's Greek cross design of the building has more height than breadth. The façade is further adorned by statues sculpted by Antonin Braun.

Like so many of Prague's religious buildings, the Church of St Nicholas fell into disrepair after Joseph II's dissolution of the monasteries in 1782, part of his reform movement for freedom of religion. The church was then used as a warehouse, apart from a brief period in the 19th century when it was occupied by the Russian Orthodox Church. As such, the interior still doesn't live up to the promise of its façade.

During World War I, however, when it was used as a garrison, an art-loving general seized the opportunity to restore some of its features, including the dome frescoes and a wonderful 19th-century chandelier of Bohemian glass. Most visitors attending one of the many summer classical music concerts are particularly captivated by the interiors. Today, the church is also the central base for the Czech Hussite Church, which has owned it since 1920.

Left: The baroque majesty of St Nicholas's Church
Above: One of the towers of the church

✚ **17 B2**

✉ **Kostel sv Mikuláše**
Staroměstské náměstí 27

☎ 224 190 991

🔲 **www.svmikulas.cz**

🕐 Tue–Fri 10–noon

✋ Free

🚇 Staroměstská

Muzeum Bedřicha Smetany

The Bedrich Smetana Museum was set up in 1936 in honour of Bedřich Smetana (1824–84), known as the father of Czech music, who to the Czech people, is their most important composer. The 19th century witnessed a second Golden Age for the country – the power of the Austro-Hungarian Empire was weakening considerably at the time when Czechs began to campaign for an independent culture.

The 1800s saw the wealth of industry arrive in the country, as well as the construction of symbolic buildings such as the National Theatre. It came to be known as the National Revival period and Smetana's music, epitomising the patriotism of Bohemia, was at the heart of it all.

Smetana's opera *Libuše*, based on Czech legends, was the opening performance at the National Theatre in

1881. Other works such as *The Bartered Bride* and in particular the *Ma Vlast* (*My Country*) symphonic cycle remain dear to the hearts of all Czechs. The latter is all the more remarkable for being completed towards the end of Smetana's life when he had become deaf following an illness.

This small museum honours the great musical patriot with displays of instruments, his conductor's baton and sheet music. It also explores 19th-century Czech music, including that of Smetana's great successors Dvořák and Janáček.

The building in which the museum is housed is worth a visit in its own right – a beautiful neo-Renaissance edifice decorated with sgraffito detailing on its façade. Smetana's tomb is located in the Czech Republic's most important cemetery in Vyšehrad.

Above left: The ornate sgraffito façade of the Bedrich Smetana Museum, which was originally the Old Town waterworks, was built on the banks of the Vltava River in the 1880s. Since 1936 it has been home to the Smetana exhibition
Above right: Ornate sgraffito decorates the upper front elevation

✠ **17 A2**

✉ **Muzeum Bedřicha Smetany**
Novotného lávka 1

☎ 222 220 082

🌐 **www.nm.cz**

🕐 Wed–Mon 10–12, 12:30–5

✋ Inexpensive

Ⓜ Staroměstská

Obecní dům

Prague's Municipal House is the cultural heartland of the city and home to its most important concert hall, dedicated to the nation's beloved composer Bedřich Smetana. The site has always been important to the city; in the Middle Ages, before the kings of Bohemia moved to their castle setting, this was the palace of the former royal family.

The original building was demolished at the turn of the 20th century and replaced with the stunning art nouveau building seen today, embodying the style that was prevalent throughout Europe at the time.

The façade is immediately recognisable by the elaborate green dome and the beautiful mosaic called *Homage to Prague*. Inside the decoration is equally breathtaking, created by some of the country's greatest artists of the early 20th century, such as Alfons Mucha.

Besides the vast Smetana Hall, there are also a number of smaller and more

intimate music venues, as well as a café that remains one of the most stunning art nouveau dining areas in the city.

The Municipal House has also played a key role in the history of the country. On 28 October, 1918, the announcement that the Czech Republic had been created was made from here; in 1989, the crucial talks between the Communist rulers and Václav Havel's Civic Forum Party were held here, resulting in the Velvet Revolution and the fall of the Communist regime.

Above: The Municipal House, built in the 20th century in the art nouveau style
Above right: The café inside is always filled with diners

✚ **17 D2**

✉ **Obecní dům**
Náměstí Republiky 5

☎ 222 002 101

www **www.obecni-dum.cz**

⏱ During concert times and for the café

✋ Free

Ⓜ Náměstí Republiky

Prašná brána

The 65m (213-foot) high Powder Gate is one of Prague's most elegant Gothic structures, built in 1475 as one of the 13 gateways into the Old Town that protected access to the royal arena. The tower was left unfinished for hundreds of years because the royal family relocated to Prague Castle and the gates became redundant.

It wasn't until the 19th century that citizens recognised the value of the craftsmanship and renovated and embellished the tower. In the 17th century it was used as a depot for storing gunpowder, hence its current name, Powder Gate. The true beauty of the tower is its exterior, which is something of a forerunner of the architecture that can be experienced throughout the Old Town. There is a permanent exhibition inside detailing the history of the city's gates. Visitors can also climb the staircase to the top of the tower for a bird's-eye view of the city.

✚ **17 D2**

✉ **Prašná brána**
   Na příkopě

☎ 724 063 723

🕓 Apr–Oct, daily 10–6

✋ Inexpensive

🚇 Náměstí Republiky

Left: The Powder Gate was a ceremonial entrance to the Old Town
Above: A view of the Old Town

Staroměstské náměstí

Undeniably the soul of the city, Prague's Old Town Square is one of the most unforgettable sights in the whole of Eastern Europe. The history and architecture that are enclosed in this relatively small space are quite simply breathtaking. The square was first constructed in the early 13th century as a centre for trade and commerce, where merchants from around the region would meet to sell their wares. It is still the most popular meeting point in the city today.

✚ **17 C2**

✉ **Staroměstské náměstí**

🚇 Staroměstská

Golz-Kinský Palace

☎ **224 810 758**

📧 **www.ngprague.cz**

🕐 Tue–Sun 10–6

✋ Moderate

At the heart of the square, invariably filled with people relaxing on its steps, is the Jan Hus Monument. Hus, considered something of a national hero, was an outspoken religious reformer who protested against the corruption he believed he witnessed within the Catholic Church.

Above: The painted calendar below the Astronomical Clock, Old Town Hall
Right: Viewed from the square, you can see the golden Virgin on the gable flanked by the twin towers on the front of the medieval Týn Church

He was eventually burned at the stake, but his followers formed the Hussite Movement that did much to alter the state of the church in the 15th century.

Apart from the two main churches on the square, there are several palaces and houses that are significant in their own right. Palác Bolz-Kinských (Golz-Kinský Palace) has one of the most beautiful façades, a rococo splendour in pink and white built in the 18th century by one of Prague's most important architects, Kilián Ignaz Dientzenhofer. The palace, now part of the National Gallery, also has a more sombre role in history – Communist leader Klement Gottwald announced the victory of his party from its balcony in 1948. Next to the Golz-Kinský Palace is a Gothic

building known as the House at the Stone Bell. It is one of many such buildings on the square and throughout the Old Town that are named after adornments and signs on their façades – in this case, clearly, a stone bell. Other houses include At the Stone Ram, At the Golden Unicorn and At the Red Fox.

House signs are also a major feature of Celetná, the important street leading off from the square on the south side. In the Middle Ages this street was a part of the royal route along which the coronation processions of Bohemian kings would pass. Today its many baroque buildings are largely occupied by shops, restaurants and streetside cafés catering to the large number of tourists that flock here every day.

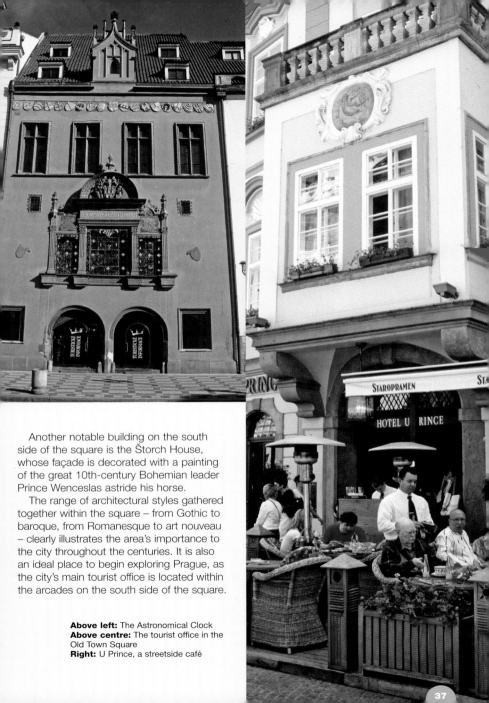

Another notable building on the south side of the square is the Štorch House, whose façade is decorated with a painting of the great 10th-century Bohemian leader Prince Wenceslas astride his horse.

The range of architectural styles gathered together within the square – from Gothic to baroque, from Romanesque to art nouveau – clearly illustrates the area's importance to the city throughout the centuries. It is also an ideal place to begin exploring Prague, as the city's main tourist office is located within the arcades on the south side of the square.

Above left: The Astronomical Clock
Above centre: The tourist office in the Old Town Square
Right: U Prince, a streetside café

Hradčany

The sight of Prague Castle and the spires of St Vitus's Cathedral looming over the city and Vltava River is one of the most striking views of any European capital. The Old Town may boast its wonderful alleyways and churches, but Hradčany is the true heart of Prague, first as home to the Bohemian monarchy and now the presidential seat and political nucleus of the nation. It can take a day or more to explore the castle complex, so packed it is with historical and architectural gems. If the pace and the crowds get too much, there are always the more tranquil settings of the Strahov Monastery or the pastel-coloured street known as Nový svět.

HRADČANY WALK

1. Pražský hrad
See page 62

The vast complex of Prague Castle dominates the city skyline, perched on a hill above the Old Town and the Vltava River. Home to the Bohemian royalty from the 9th century, it was also the residence of the presidency following the foundation of the Czechoslovak Republic in 1918. At its heart is the impressive cathedral of St Vitus.

2. Arcibiskupský palác
See page 42

Directly in front of the entrance to Prague Castle is the Archbishop's Palace, dating from the 16th century. The interior, still the seat of the Czech archbishop, is closed to the public, but the striking rococo façade makes it more than worth a visit.

3. Šternberský palác
See page 68

Behind the Archbishop's Palace is Sternberg Palace, which has been home to a growing collection of art since the 18th century. Begun as a private venture, the collection is now run by the Czech government. Highlights include works by Picasso, Rembrandt and Chagall. Walk down Kanovnická to Nový svět.

4. Nový svět
See page 60

Literally translated as "New World", this short street was once home to staff and servants of the royal household at Prague Castle. The houses are therefore small and humble, yet wonderfully picturesque with their pastel shades and intricate house signs. At the end of Nový svět, turn left on to Černinská. Walk to the end of this road.

5. Loretánská kaple
See page 56

This chapel is dedicated to the legend of the Santa Casa. It is claimed that the Angel Gabriel forewarned Mary here about the impending birth of her son, Jesus. The house was later moved from Israel to the Italian town of Loreta. The Cloisters and complex are a masterful illustration of baroque architecture at its finest.

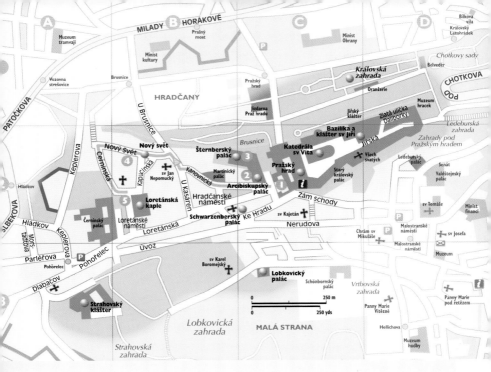

Arcibiskupský palác

The Archbishop's Palace, just in front of the castle gateway, has been the seat of the city's archbishopric since 1562. Earlier, the archbishops had resided in the Malá Strana district, but that residence had been destroyed during the Hussite Wars of the 15th century.

Moving the archbishopric so close to the royal residence was a gesture to indicate the importance of the Catholic faith to the Czech people. Because it remains the archbishop's residence to this day, the interior is closed to the public, but the beautiful façade is definitely worth a look. The white rococo design was the result of renovations at the end of the 18th century when baroque was overwhelmingly

changing the face of much of European architecture. Also on the façade is a coat of arms depicting the archbishop, in a green hat with 10 tassels, with the lesser officials surrounding him. In front of the palace gates is an elaborate statue of warring Titans.

Above left: Detail of the ornate coat of arms added in 1764–65 by J J Wirch (1538–64) on the Archbishop's Palace
Above right: Sightseers in the forecourt beneath the restored rococo façade

✚ **41 C2**

✉ **Arcibiskupský palác**
Hradčanské náměstí 16

🚫 Closed to the public

Ⓜ Malostranská or Hradčanská

Bazilika sv Jiří

The Basilica of St George is the oldest surviving church in Prague, dating
from the early 10th century when it was founded by Prince Vratislav I.
The Romanesque-style building seen today, however, dates from 1142
when the church was rebuilt following a fire that destroyed much of
the original structure. Over the centuries, the basilica has been much
enlarged and renovated, including the baroque adornment of the façade
in the 18th century. The interior, however, remains firmly Romanesque in
appearance, its stark atmosphere quite at odds with more flamboyant
religious buildings around the city.

Above left: Exterior of the basilica
Above right: The National Gallery's
collection in the adjoining convent

Inside the church are the tombs of many kings of the Přemyslid dynasty that dominated Bohemia in the Middle Ages, including that of Vratislav himself. There is also a chapel dedicated to St Ludmilla, which contains her tomb. The grandmother of Prince Wenceslas, she became a martyr when she was murdered by her jealous daughter-in-law while at prayer.

There is also a chapel dedicated to St John Nepomuk, the canonised vicar who was murdered by the king's troops in the 14th century. The basilica's interior boasts wonderful acoustics, largely due to its lack of adornment, and is therefore a popular choice for classical concerts, particularly in summer.

✝ **41 C2**

✉ **Bazilika sv Jiří**
Náměstí U Svatého Jiří

☎ Church: 224 373 368
Gallery: 257 531 644

🌐 Church: **www.hrad.cz**
Gallery: **www.ngprague.cz**

🕐 Daily 9–5 (gallery closes at 4 Nov–Mar)

✋ Church free; gallery moderate

Ⓜ Malostranská or Hradčanská

Next door to the basilica is St George's Convent (Klášter sv Jiří), the first of its kind in Bohemia, established in AD 973 by Prince Boleslav and his sister Mlada for the Benedictine order of nuns. It remained a working convent until the dissolution of all convents and monasteries in 1782 by Emperor Joseph II. The building was later used as military barracks, but in the 1970s the authorities decided to utilise the former convent to house the National Gallery's collection of Czech art from the 12th to the 18th centuries, focusing specifically on Gothic, Mannerist and baroque works.

The result is one of the finest art galleries in Prague. Highlights of the chronologically arranged collection include the strikingly modern-looking St Elizabeth panel (1360) by Master Theodoric, and the powerful

Tobias Restoring His Father's Sight (1705) by Petr Brandl. There are also sculpted works by Peter Parler, the great stonemason who embellished so much of the city in his day. Most of the Mannerist works, such as *The Last Judgement* by Josef Heintz, date from the reign of Emperor Rudolf II (1583–1612), who far preferred painting to politics and turned Prague briefly into a pilgrimage site for artists from around Europe.

Left: *St John of Nepomuk* (18th century, anon) in St George's Convent
Above: St George's Convent and Basilica present different faces
Right: *Crucifixion of St Andrew* by Michael Leopold Willman in the convent

Katedrála sv Víta

St Vitus's Cathedral is the most important religious building in Prague and dominates the skyline of the Hradčany area. There had been a church on this site since the 10th century, but the spectacular Gothic building seen today owes its presence to Charles IV, the Holy Roman Emperor who changed so much of the face of Prague during his reign. The great medieval architects Peter Parler and Matthias of Arras were commissioned to work on the cathedral from 1344 onwards, but work was constantly disrupted over the centuries, largely due to religious wars.

Above left: St Vitus's in the early evening
Above right: The Golden Portal and bell tower

The cathedral building was completed only in 1929 after a late 19th-century push by the National Revival movement. The most dominant features of the façade are the elaborately carved twin spires, the Renaissance bell tower and beautiful 10m (33-foot) long rose window with its stained-glass interpretations of biblical scenes. Take time, however, to wander the entire length of the façade to admire the masterful flying buttresses and the often humorous gargoyles that peer out from their rooftop perches.

The official main entrance is the Golden Portal, which forms part of the original 14th-century building, although today this is reserved only for state occasions. The

✠ **41 C2**

✉ **Katedrála sv Víta**
   Pražský hrad – III nádvoří

☎ 257 531 622

🌐 **www.katedralapraha.cz**

🕐 Mar–Oct, Mon–Sat 9–5, Sun 12–5;
   Nov–Feb, Mon–Sat 9–4, Sun 12–4

✋ Free

Ⓜ Malostranská

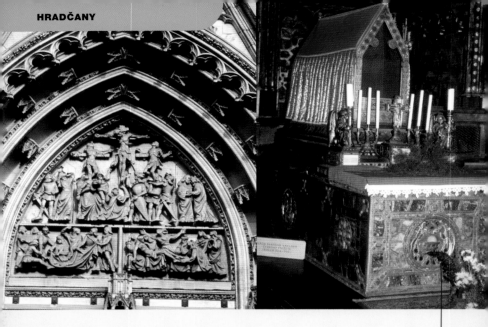

public main entrance is now on the west side of the building, marked by a bronze door that celebrates the stories of saints Wenceslas and Adalbert.

Inside, the cathedral is as striking as its façade. The most important area is the Chapel of St Wenceslas, built in 929 by Prince Wenceslas, in which his tomb, adorned with gemstones, has an overwhelming presence. It is surmounted with a golden steeple and is stunningly decorated with frescoes depicting the life of the saint, as well as scenes from the Bible, including Christ's crucifixion. If any proof was needed of how much the Czechs revere the unfortunate 10th-century prince and their patron saint, this is it. Legend has it that the lion-head doorknocker on the entrance to the chapel is the one that he clung to when he was brutally murdered by his brother Boleslav. A passage within the chapel leads to a chamber which houses the Bohemian Crown Jewels.

The cathedral is also the burial place of many of the Bohemian rulers, in the Royal Mausoleum and the crypt, which contain the tomb of the building's founder Charles IV, as well as that of Emperor Rudolf II. But there are many more highlights. The chancel, with its wonderful vaulted ceiling, is one of the masterpieces of Peter Parler's work in Prague. The tomb of St John Nepomuk is a striking work of carved silver. Much of the stained glass is in marked contrast to the rest of the cathedral as it dates from the 20th century, but it is spectacular none-the-less. It includes a depiction of St Cyril and St Methodius by the admired art nouveau artist Alfons Mucha. The choir area has remarkable intricate woodcarvings; one depicts the city in astonishing detail just as it was during the 17th century.

Above left: Detail of the cathedral's west façade
Above right: St Wenceslas's tomb;
Right: Alfons Mucha's stunning stained-glass window in the New Archbishops' Chapel

Královská zahrada

To the north of the castle complex is the most important green area, the Royal Gardens. They were laid out in 1534 on the orders of Ferdinand I, who was keen to add a Renaissance-style garden to the castle's recreational areas. The Royal Summer House (or Belvedere) is decorated with mythological figures. There is also a Ball Game Pavilion, which was once the tennis court where the nobility played. The Lion Court now houses an attractive restaurant, but its name recalls the time when the ever-eccentric Rudolf II kept a zoo here with lions, tigers and bears.

Above left: A garden pavilion
Above right: *The Allegory of Night* by Antonin Braun outside the Ball Game Hall

Over the centuries the gardens were used to grow rare and exotic plants brought back from expeditions abroad – tulips may be associated with Holland today, but they were first introduced here from the Middle East during the reign of Ferdinand I. A great deal of the gardens were re-landscaped in the 19th century following the then popular English style.

The gardens are separated from the castle by the Stag Moat, where game was once kept ready for royal hunts. In summer the gardens are often crowded as both locals and visitors to the city come for a stroll among the blooms, away from the packed cobbled streets around the neighbouring castle.

✛ **41 C1**

✉ **Královská zahrada**
U Prašného mostu

☎ 224 373 579

🔳 **www.hrad.cz**

🕓 Tue–Sun 10–6

💳 Free, charge for exhibitions in Ball Game Pavilion

Ⓜ Malostranská or Hradčanská

Lobkovický palác

Lobkowicz Palace stands at the eastern end of the castle complex and dates from around 1570, when its four wings and courtyard were home to the important Pernstejn aristocracy. The sgraffito decoration on the façade is original, although like so much of Prague the house was greatly altered during the baroque period when it became the residence of the noble Lobkowicz family. Little of what was originally a private house, however, now remains inside, apart from the banqueting hall decorated with impressive frescoes and the chapel.

Above: In an overall view of the palace its white mass stands out against the red-tiled rooftops

The rest of Lobkowicz Palace has been given over to a museum (part of the National Museum collection) documenting various moments in Czech history through artworks, sculpture, weaponry, religious artefacts and altars rescued from churches around the city. There are also copies of the Bohemian Crown Jewels here. It's all rather eclectic and possibly appeals to only those with a strong interest in Bohemian history, but it's worth a look to soak up the atmosphere of a wealthy 17th-century home. A little further along, on Zlatá ulička Daliborky, is the Dalibor Tower which served as a prison between the 15th and 18th centuries. It was named after its original inmate whose story inspired Bedřich Smetana's opera of the same name.

✝ **41 C3**

✉ **Lobkovický palác**
Jiřská 3

☎ Palace: 602 595 998
Museum: 257 534 578

🌐 **www.nm.cz**

🕓 Tue–Sun 10–6

✋ Inexpensive

Ⓜ Malostranská

Loretánská kaple

This wonderful baroque edifice, recognisable by its white façade and green-domed bell towers, was built in 1626 to bring the rather bizarre legend of the Santa Casa to Prague and the Czech people.

✚ **41 B2**

✉ **Loretánská kaple**
Loretánské náměstí 7

☎ **220 516 740**

🔤 **www.loreta.cz**

🕓 Tue–Sun 9–12:15, 1–4:30

✋ Moderate

🚇 Malostranská

The Santa Casa was thought to be the house where the Archangel Gabriel appeared to the Virgin Mary to tell her about the impending birth of Jesus. In the Middle Ages the Holy House was carried by two monks from Israel, where it was under threat from Muslim invaders, first to Dalmatia and then to the Italian town of Loreta. With the Catholic resurgence of the 17th century, the legend grew in popularity and this grand celebration of the cult was commissioned by the noblewoman Kateřina of Lobkowicz,

Above: The baroque exterior of the Loreta Church
Right: The bell tower soars high above the treetops

who ordered the construction of a replica of the house here. Architecturally the most striking aspect of the complex is the baroque cloisters, designed by a definitive artist of the era, Kilián Ignaz Dientzenhofer. The Loreta soon became a very important pilgrimage site and the enclosures were intended to protect the devout from the ravages of the Prague climate. Sadly, the artworks decorating the ceilings of the cloisters have not stood the test of time well.

Within the cloisters are six small chapels dedicated to various saints, while within each courtyard are beautifully sculpted fountains depicting aspects of Mary's life. Less appealing is the Church of the Nativity in which several skeletons, gruesomely dressed in human clothing, are placed. If you can overlook this fact, however, the church is a veritable explosion of baroque artistry, from its frescoes to its golden altar. It was created in 1717 by Christoph Dientzenhofer out of the existing chapel of St Anne at the Loreta sanctuary.

Apart from the Santa Casa, decorated with reliefs depicting the story of the Madonna, the most important area of the Loreta is the treasury. Various liturgical artefacts rescued from other churches and cathedrals are stored here, notably the beautiful monstrance known as the Prague Sun. Weighing around 12kg (27 pounds) and decorated with gold and more than 6,000 diamonds, it's possibly the most valuable religious item in the city.

The 27 bells of the main tower at the front of the complex, known as the carillon, ring out on the hour every hour between 9am and 6pm. Unsurprisingly there is a legend surrounding this, too. During a plague epidemic in the city, one mother watched helplessly as one after another

each of her children fell victim to the disease, and on the death of each she asked for the Loreta bells to be rung. When she herself died it's said that the bells miraculously rang in mourning of their own accord. Hence, the regular hourly chorus since that day of a hymn to Mary known as "We Greet Thee a Thousand Times".

Above left: Guilded decoration surrounds pink marble columns in the Church of the Nativity
Above right: A view of the upper façade
Right: The covered passageway is lined with period furniture and frescoes decorating the vaults

Nový svět

Meaning "New World", Nový svět was once the slum area of Hradčany and was where the workers and staff of Prague Castle and the royal household lived. The area was susceptible to fires, the last of which, in 1541, pretty much destroyed most of it.

Many of the homes that are seen today date from the 18th century and their pretty pastel-coloured façades are a far cry from the dirty lanes that once made up the area. Following a long-standing Prague tradition, descriptive house names rather than numbers, identify the houses, such as The Golden Foot, The Golden Star and The Golden Pear, now converted into a wine bar. It's a part of the city that continues to attract artists and writers particularly, and anyone searching for a quiet stroll away from the bustle of the cobbled streets around the castle proper.

At the top of the street is Černínský palác (Černín Palace), a beautiful baroque building (not open to the public) decorated with columns that was once home to the wealthy Černín family. Its most notorious moment in history came in the 20th century. When the Communist regime came to power in 1948 the only non-Communist in the government, Jan Masaryk, was found dead, having apparently fallen from a top-floor window of the building. Speculation still reigns as to whether he was murdered, particularly in a city with a long tradition of defenestration as punishment for perceived sins and crimes.

Left: View down the cobbled, winding Černínská street in Nový svět quarter, whose rustic appearance has a charm of its own
Above right: A powerful statue of St John Nepomuk on top of a wall on Černínská street

✚ **41 B2**
✉ **Nový svět**
Ⓜ Malastranská

Pražský hrad

The symbol of the nation, Prague Castle, perched on its hill above the Vltava, has been the centre of government for centuries, first of the monarchy and, from 1918 onwards, the presidential office. The long history of this large complex, beginning in the 9th century, can be discerned at almost every turn in the varying architectural styles, each representing a different era.

Apart from St Vitus's Cathedral, the most important building here is the Royal Palace (Královský palác), home to the Bohemian royalty from the 11th century onwards. Its most impressive room, through its sheer size, is the Vladislav Hall, constructed with a vast vaulted roof in the 15th century.

The hall is so large that indoor jousts were staged here, competitors accessing the hall via the wide Riders' Staircase.

One of the most famous moments in Prague history occurred at the palace in 1618 when a large crowd of Protestant protestors stormed the building to confront

three Catholic governors. After a struggle the three were thrown out of a window but miraculously survived by falling directly on to a soft dung heap below. Known as the "second defenstration" of Prague, this event marks the onset of the Thirty Years War. In the so-called "New Palace" are the spectacular Spanish Hall and Rudolf's Gallery, with baroque excesses in their white and gold decoration. The rooms are now used for state occasions and are only open to the public twice a year on 8 May and 28 October, both public holidays celebrating freedom from oppression.

Above: Prague Castle, floodlit by night, watches over the city, with St Vitus's Cathedral in the background

✚ **41 C2**

✉ **Pražský hrad**

☎ 224 371 111

🔡 **www.hrad.cz**

🕐 Daily: castle complex Apr–Oct, 5am–midnight; Nov–Mar 6am–11pm. Interior buildings: Apr–Oct, 9–5; Nov–Mar, 9–4. Changing of the Guard every hour Apr–Oct, 5am–midnight; Nov–Mar, 6am–11pm

✋ Buildings moderate; grounds free

Ⓜ Hradčanská or Malostranská

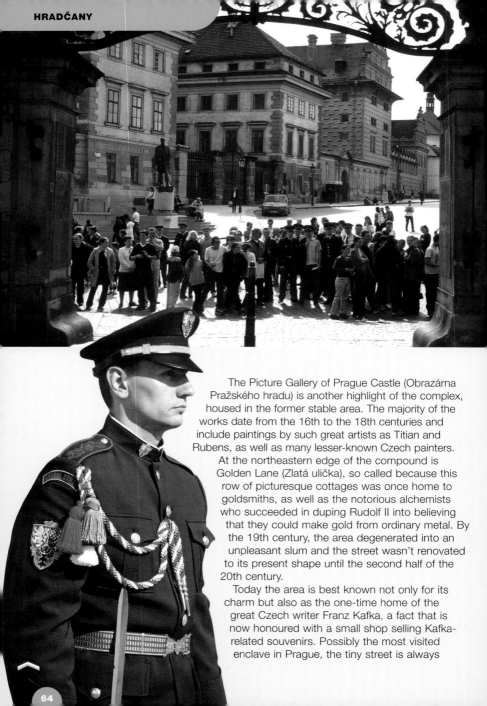

The Picture Gallery of Prague Castle (Obrazárna Pražského hradu) is another highlight of the complex, housed in the former stable area. The majority of the works date from the 16th to the 18th centuries and include paintings by such great artists as Titian and Rubens, as well as many lesser-known Czech painters. At the northeastern edge of the compound is Golden Lane (Zlatá ulička), so called because this row of picturesque cottages was once home to goldsmiths, as well as the notorious alchemists who succeeded in duping Rudolf II into believing that they could make gold from ordinary metal. By the 19th century, the area degenerated into an unpleasant slum and the street wasn't renovated to its present shape until the second half of the 20th century.

Today the area is best known not only for its charm but also as the one-time home of the great Czech writer Franz Kafka, a fact that is now honoured with a small shop selling Kafka-related souvenirs. Possibly the most visited enclave in Prague, the tiny street is always

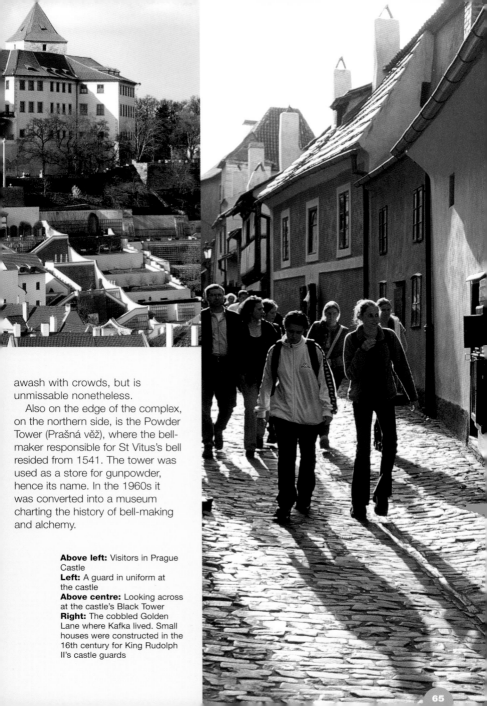

awash with crowds, but is unmissable nonetheless.

Also on the edge of the complex, on the northern side, is the Powder Tower (Prašná věž), where the bell-maker responsible for St Vitus's bell resided from 1541. The tower was used as a store for gunpowder, hence its name. In the 1960s it was converted into a museum charting the history of bell-making and alchemy.

Above left: Visitors in Prague Castle
Left: A guard in uniform at the castle
Above centre: Looking across at the castle's Black Tower
Right: The cobbled Golden Lane where Kafka lived. Small houses were constructed in the 16th century for King Rudolph II's castle guards

Schwarzenberský palác

The architectural decoration known as sgraffito, when one layer of plaster is scraped away to reveal patterns of a different coloured plaster beneath, was very popular in Prague in the 16th century, and the façade of the Schwarzenberg Palace is one of the finest examples of this technique. Originally built in the Italian Renaissance style between 1545 and 1576, the palace was finally bought by the noble Schwarzenberg family in the 18th century, from whom it takes its name.

Today the palace is not only of architectural appeal but a draw to anyone with an interest in warfare, as it is now home to the Museum of Military History (Vojenské historické museum). The region once known as Bohemia has witnessed centuries of armed struggles, from the religious Hussite Wars and Thirty Years War to the world wars of the 20th century, so this is a full and fascinating collection. The stories of all these battles are conveyed through displays of uniforms, weapons, documents and other paraphernalia. This collection only covers the period from the Middle Ages to 1918 – later military history is explored in a second museum in the suburb of Žižkov to the east of the city centre.

Left: Several large field guns are displayed in the paved, arcaded forecourt of the Military Museum, housed in the sgraffito-decorated Schwarzenberg Palace
Above: Detail of one of the ornately decorated ceilings within the palace

✚ **41 C2**

✉ **Schwarzenberský palác**
Hradčanské náměstí 2

☎ 202 020 20

🕐 May–Oct, Tue–Sun 10–6

✋ Inexpensive, Tue free

Ⓜ Malostranská

Šternberský palác

The baroque Sternberg Palace is a delight in itself, but it is also home to the National Gallery's (Národní galerie) impressive collection of European art from the 14th to the 18th centuries. The building has a long connection with the art world: in the late 18th century the palace's owner, Franz Josef Sternberg, founded an art society here to which fellow aristocrats donated works from their private collections. The wealth of art began to grow and both the building and the collection were donated to the state in 1949 to allow them to be on public display. The collection was also reviewed and revised in 2003 to present its current permanent exhibition.

Above: Exterior of the 18th-century Sternberg Palace which houses the National Gallery's collection of European art, donated by the wealthy residents of the time

The works here are arranged according to country of origin and the periods in which they were created. On the first floor there are some wonderful and priceless pieces from ancient Greece, Rome and Egypt, as well as beautiful Italian religious art from the medieval period, such as the *Lamentation of Christ* by Florentine artist Lorenzo Monaco. The second floor contains fabulous works by artists whose names are renowned the world over, from Spain, France and Italy as well as Flemish and Dutch masters. Here you can find *Head of Christ* by the Spanish artist El Greco and *View of the Thames* by the great Venetian master Canaletto, among many other treasures. Rembrandt, Rubens and Goya all have works in this part of the gallery.

The ground floor focuses on German art between the 16th and 18th centuries,

Above: Gallery of German paintings with Albrecht Dürer's *Feast of the Rosary* to the left in the picture

✚ **41 B2**

✉ **Šternberský palác**
Hradčanské náměstí 15

☎ 233 090 570

🔳 **www.ngprague.cz**

🕓 Tue–Sun 10–6 (first Wed of the month 10–8)

✋ Moderate, free first Wed of the month 3–8pm

Ⓜ Malostranská or Hradčanská

which was a particular passion of the great art collector Rudolf II. The highlight here is the *Feast of the Rosary* by German master Albrecht Dürer. Rudolf was so impassioned with this particular painting that he personally oversaw its transportation from Venice to Prague.

Throughout the collections there are also many sculptural pieces from each individual period. Don't forget to look at the interior architecture of the palace itself. Many of the ceilings still boast original frescoes, and the Chinese Room has some wonderful chinoiserie decoration on its walls. There's also a comprehensive library, open to the public, which contains a good collection of art books and periodicals.

At one time the Sternberg Palace also housed more modern works from the 19th and 20th centuries, but the sheer size of the collection required extra space and these are now on display in the Veletržní palác (Trade Fair Palace), a rather functional and unappealing building in the Letná district northeast of the city centre.

Left: A visitor admires the work of Cranach the Elder in the gallery of German paintings
Above left: *St Bruno* by van Dyck
Above right: Wide-open spaces help observers to appreciate the paintings in the Flemish and Dutch gallery

Strahovský klášter

Strahov Monastery was originally founded in the 12th century by an order known as the Premonstratensian monks. A little over 100 years later a fire ravaged the once-Romanesque building. What is seen today is a blend of Gothic and baroque styles following the subsequent rebuilding and renovation that took place.

Strahov continued to be a working monastery until the advent of the Communist regime in 1948, but it is best known today for its library, which escaped the dissolution of the monasteries, that took place throughout Bohemia in 1782. The Theological Hall and the Philosophical Hall are the main areas of the library. The latter boasts a wonderful ceiling fresco by Anton Maulbertsch depicting great thinkers in history, which looms down over old wooden bookcases packed with priceless religious works. The former also features frescoes, this time with more of a religious theme, as well as a collection of rare 17th-century astronomical globes. Among the thousands

of titles held in the collection, the most valuable is undoubtedly the *Strahov Gospel*, a beautiful 9th-century manuscript. Another part of the library is the Museum of National Literature, whose collection focuses on Czech works from the 19th and 20th centuries and the National Revival period.

Also within the complex is the wonderfully baroque Church of Our Lady. The church still has the original organ on which Mozart played during his time in Prague.

Above left: Entrance to the Strahov Monastery
Above right: The rare 9th-century *Strahov Gospel*, with its richly bejewelled cover

✚ **41 A3**

✉ **Strahovský klášter**
Strahovské nádvoří 1

☎ 233 107 711

🌐 **www.strahovskyklaster.cz**

🕐 Tue–Sun 9–12, 1–5

✋ Inexpensive

🚌 22

Josefov

The Jewish community had suffered persecution and segregation for centuries throughout Europe, often forced to live in ghettos. Prague's ghetto in the Josefov area was one of the earliest, dating from the 11th century. While they could work and live together in this area, there were strict rules about travelling to other parts of the city. The situation lasted until 1848, when the segregation laws were abandoned as part of the National Revival movement, but freedom was to be short-lived. In 1939 the Nazis occupied Prague and by 1941 almost the entire Jewish community was deported to concentration camps. Few returned, but those who did still maintain the Jewish area with much pride. Steven Spielberg used the streets of the Josefov area to re-create the Warsaw ghetto in the Academy Award-winning film *Schindler's List*.

JOSEFOV WALK

1. Anežský klášter
See page 78

This wonderful Gothic building is now a branch of the Czech National Gallery, specialising in Czech art, which compares well to many famous artists' work on show in Europe. Walk down U milosrdných, turn left down Dlouha kozi and right on to Bílkova. At the end of this road turn left on to Pařížská.

2. Staronová synagoga
See page 90

A true survivor, the Old-New Synagogue is the most important Jewish building in Prague. The interior is an impressive collection of vaulting, columns and chandeliers, while a beautiful Ark contains the Jewish Torah. Turn right on to Červená, the square on the northwest side.

3. Vysoká synagoga
See page 100

The Jewish Quarter's High Synagogue dates from the late 16th century and was originally joined with the Jewish Town Hall. It is still a working synagogue and has a fine collection of Jewish religious items, including beautiful menorahs and mantles. Continue down Červená and turn right on to U Starého hřbitova.

4. Starý židovský hřbitov
See page 94

All graveyards have an understandably melancholy air, but the Jewish Cemetery of Prague is particularly moving for the vast number of crumbling graves that are piled up in the only space allotted for Jewish burials from the 15th to the 18th centuries. Many of Prague's most notable Jewish figures have their last resting place here.

5. Uměleckoprůmyslové muzeum
See page 98

Prague's Museum of Decorative Arts, known familiarly as the UPM, gives fitting emphasis to the world-renowned Bohemian glass, but there is much more here besides, including pottery, ceramics, furniture, fashion, photography and tapestry.

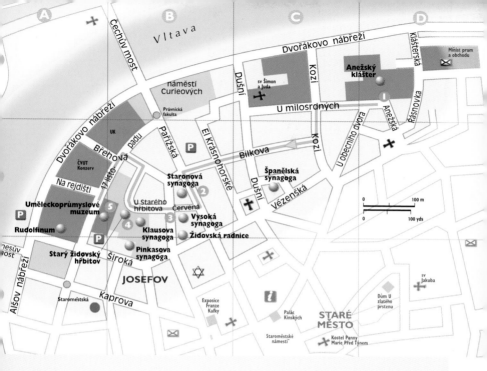

Anežský klášter

The Convent of St Agnes is named after Agnes, daughter of Otakar I and the sister of Wenceslas I. She founded a religious order of Poor Clare nuns here in the 13th century, and the convent was built in 1233. Construction work on the church continued until 1280. The wonderful Gothic building was deserted, following the dissolution of the monasteries and convents by Josef II in 1782 and, like so many of the city's religious buildings, saw centuries of neglect and dilapidation, the area becoming little more than a slum.

In the 1960s, however, and again in 2000, the convent was renovated and is now home to the country's most important

Left and above: The Church of St Francis of Assisi on the premises of St Agnes Convent in the Josefov area

✚ **77 C1**

✉ **Anežský klášter**
U milosrdných 17

☎ 224 810 628

🌐 **www.ngprague.cz**

🕐 Tue–Sun 10–6

✋ Moderate

Ⓜ Staroměstská or Náměstí Republiky

collection of Czech art from the 14th to the 16th centuries under one roof. It forms part of the National Gallery's collection that is spread over various buildings in and outside the city centre.

The Middle Ages were something of a Golden Age for Bohemian art, because the painters of the day began to bring a new sense of realism to previously stylised religious imagery, hence the importance of this collection. There are three main artists that dominate the works of this period in Bohemia: Master Theodoric, Master of the Vyšší Brod and Master of the Třeboň Altar.

As the works move towards the Renaissance period, it's clear that neighbouring European countries were beginning to exert their influence here, too, and the collection also features works by German and Austrian artists such as Lucas Cranach the Elder.

The building contains the tombs of Agnes and Wenceslas I. Agnes was canonised in 1989 on Pope John Paul II's first visit to the Czech capital.

Left: Works of art in the Convent of St Agnes
Above: The vaulted cloister, the oldest remaining Gothic building in Prague
Right: St Agnes comes to life in an expressive sculpture in the convent

Klausová synagoga

The original site of the Klausen Synagogue was made up of a collection of small buildings used for prayer and education, established by the Jewish mayor Mordechai Maisel in the 16th century. In 1689 these buildings were ravaged by fire and a new synagogue was erected on the site in baroque style, which eventually became the largest synagogue in the area that was known as the Prague Ghetto.

Today the building is home to a permanent collection that examines and explores the various aspects of Jewish customs and traditions, particularly in the context of day-to-day life rather than high religious orders and philosophical tenets. Explanations are given about circumcision, bar and bat mitzvah celebrations, weekly Sabbath dinners, kosher food and more.

The exhibits continue beyond the synagogue into the adjoining Romanesque-style Ceremonial Hall that was once home

to the Prague Burial Society, whose duty it was to ensure all Jewish deceased were buried according to the rituals and traditions of the Jewish faith. There are also exhibits about many of the people who shaped and assisted the Jewish community in Prague, as well as a collection of religious artefacts, including some ancient Hebrew manuscripts.

Above left: Tombstones fill the Old Jewish Cemetery at the Klausen Synagogue
Above right: Souvenir stalls in a market near the synagogue

✚ **77 B2**

✉ **Klausová synagoga**
U Starého hřbitova 1

☎ 222 310 302

🌐 **www.jewishmuseum.cz**

🕐 Apr–Oct, Sun–Fri 9–6; Nov–Mar, Sun–Fri 9–4:30

✋ Expensive

Ⓜ Staroměstská

Pinkasova synagoga

The Pinkas Synagogue was originally founded in 1479 by a rabbi of the same name, but it was some 50 years later that the building, with its Gothic ceiling, took shape. It was later expanded upon and renovated many times over the centuries.

This synagogue is the most moving monument in the Jewish Quarter, commemorating as it does the almost 80,000 Jewish people of Czechoslovakia who were deported and exterminated by the Nazis during World War II.

From the 11th century, the Jewish community of Prague had to live and work in the ghetto until 1848, when they were allowed the freedom of the city. But such freedom, so long in coming, would not last even a century. Hitler and his Nazi forces occupied Czechoslovakia in 1939 and from then on, the Jewish community was

at first re-segregated and victimised, and then, in 1941, permanently removed as part of the chilling "Final Solution". Almost all those living in the Prague Ghetto were taken to the concentration camp of Terezín (Theresienstadt) in Bohemia. From here a large majority were transported to the gas chambers of Auschwitz-Birkenau in Poland.

A decade after these atrocities, the Pinkas Synagogue was selected as a memorial site, and the walls of the building were painted with the names and places of each one of the victims. This intricate work suffered when after another decade

the walls became damp, and the memorial was closed for many years, not least because the Communists then in power showed little interest in assisting or funding the restoration. Nevertheless, following the Velvet Revolution, the work was finally completed and the memorial re-opened in 1992. Today it remains one of the most emotional parts of any visit to Prague, as visitor upon visitor ponders each name in silence.

Perhaps even more heartbreaking is a separate part of the exhibition that displays paintings by the children deported to Terezín. Their names and death dates, if known, are given alongside these naïve works of art.

A much more positive aspect of the Pinkas Synagogue was that during the restoration work in the 1970s and 1980s various details of the original medieval ghetto were excavated, including a *mikva* (ancient ritual bath).

Above left: The *bimah* in the Pinkas Synagogue
Above: While at Terezín the children drew pictures, some of which have survived

✝ **77 B3**

✉ **Pinkasova synagoga**
Široká 3

☎ 222 326 660

🌐 **www.jewishmuseum.cz**

🕐 Apr–Oct, Sun–Fri 9–6; Nov–Mar, Sun–Fri 9–4:30

✋ Expensive

Ⓜ Staroměstská

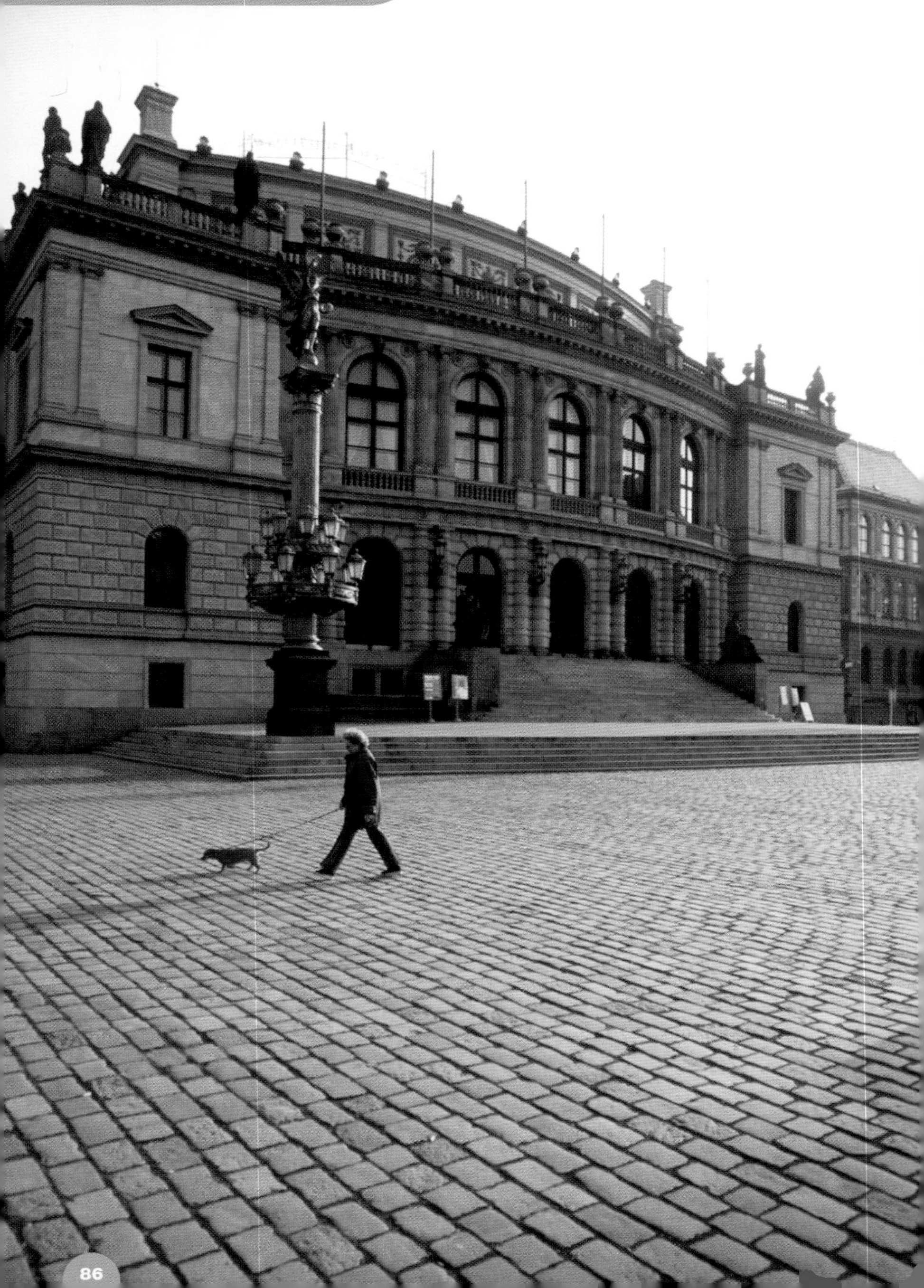

Rudolfinum

One of the most beautiful buildings to grace the banks of the Vltava River is the neo-Renaissance Rudolfinum, home to the Czech Philharmonic Orchestra since the end of World War II.

The concert hall first opened in 1885 at the height of the National Revival movement and was named after Crown Prince Rudolf. Its beautiful façade and parts of the foyer are decorated with busts and statues of the great and the good of Czech arts. The building was originally intended as an art gallery as well as a concert venue, until the National Gallery secured more permanent exhibition spaces elsewhere, and it is now occasionally used for temporary exhibitions.

The heart of the building is the Dvořák Hall, named after the revered Czech composer. The acoustics of the hall are considered so superior that the venue is often rented out to record film soundtracks of big-budget Hollywood blockbusters. This is the main setting for the renowned Prague Spring International Music Festival held every year in May, during which time classical musicians from all over the world descend on the city. The more intimate Suk Hall is used for events such as chamber music recitals.

From 1918 to 1939 and again in 1945 to 1946, troubled years for those living in Europe, the Rudolfinum was also the temporary home of the Czechoslovak government.

Left: Entrance to the Rudolfinum, home to the Czech Philharmonic Orchestra
Above: Statues of famous composers look down in a proprietorial manner from atop the Rudolfinum

⊞ **77 A2**

✉ **Rudolfinum**
Alšovo nábřeží 12

☎ 227 059 227

▥ **www.czechphilharmonic.cz**

🎫 Open for concerts and events

✋ Moderate to expensive

Ⓜ Staroměstská

Španělská synagoga

The Spanish Synagogue, dating from the 1860s, takes its name from the rather incongruous architectural style of its façade, resembling the

Moorish detailing of the Alhambra in southern Spain. These Arab-style details continue in the interior of the building. The Moors and Jewish people lived together harmoniously in Spain until they were both expelled from the country in 1492, so this may in some way be a homage to that historic coexistence. The synagogue may be relatively new in the Jewish Quarter, but it was built atop the one-time Old School, Prague's first synagogue.

The building is now home to the ever-expanding Jewish Museum of Prague and its admirable attempts to keep the history of the city's Jewish community alive. In this part of the museum, the exhibits date from the emancipation of the Jewish community in the mid-19th century, when segregation was abolished, through to the present day, including the harrowing details of World War II.

Exhibits covering the early history of the Jewish community can be found in the nearby Maisel Synagogue on Maiselova. In the former prayer hall there is a lovely collection of religious silver artefacts rescued from other synagogues around the region.

🕂 **77 C2**

✉ **Španělská synagoga**
Vězeňská 1

☎ 224 819 464

🔲 **www.jewishmuseum.cz**

🕐 Apr–Oct, Sun–Fri 9–6;
Nov–Mar, Sun–Fri 9–4:30

✋ Expensive

Ⓜ Staroměstská

Above: The exterior design of the Spanish Synagogue is reminiscent of Moorish architecture
Right: Geometric patterns decorate the interior of the synagogue

Staronová synagoga

Originally called the New Synagogue, the Old-New Synagogue got its current name when a later place of worship was constructed near by. The oldest surviving synagogue in Europe, dating from 1270, this building has withstood political upheaval, the inevitable risks from fire and various other threats to its existence. It is the most important Jewish building in Prague today and is still actively used for prayer and services. Among its more famous worshippers in history was the writer Franz Kafka.

Above left: Chandeliers softly illuminate the altar
Above right: The Romanesque gabled roof differs from the design of other Prague synagogues

Although recognisable by its gabled roof, it is the interior of the synagogue, dimly lit by elaborate chandeliers hanging from a beautiful vaulted ceiling, that is its most fascinating aspect. Outside, in a small patch of green, the sculpted figure of a dreaming Moses shows the patriarch in an unusual posture.

The most important section inside is known as the Ark, topped by a carved tympanum, which houses the Torah scrolls as well as the chief rabbi's chair that once belonged to Rabbi Löw. The 16th-century rabbi is much revered in Prague as he was thought to have had magical powers and used them to create his own personal "servant" known as the Golem, made out of mud. According to legend, the Golem was

✚ **77 B2**

✉ **Staronová synagoga**
Červená 2

☎ 221 711 511

▥ **www.jewishmuseum.cz**

🕐 Apr–Oct, Sun–Fri 9:30–6; Nov–Mar, Sun–Thu 9:30–5, Fri 9:30–2

✋ Expensive

Ⓜ Staroměstská

Left: The *almenar*, surrounded by a 15th-century wrought-iron grille and a banner gifted by Emperor Ferdinand III above
Above: A verdisgris-streaked sculpture of *Moses Dreaming of Adam* (1905) by the Czech sculptor Frantisek Bilek

a loyal if slightly mischievous companion until he eventually went mad and Löw was forced to destroy him and hide him in the attic of the synagogue. A fun, but rather nonsensical tale, it is typical of the mysticism of the age.

Also important is the Jewish Standard bearing the Star of David. Despite having to live in a ghettoised community the Jewish people were given permission to fly their own flag in the 14th century, an offer they adopted proudly. The flag hangs above the wrought-iron stage known as a *bimah* from which the cantor delivers the service. The

Star of David, a symbol of the community, also features on Rabbi Löw's chair.

Note the small window slits on either side of the naves, separating the main hall from two side corridors. These were an 18th-century addition so that previously banned female members of the community could also now participate in the services. According to Orthodox Jewish faith, women are never permitted within the main hall and usually have an upstairs gallery from which to pray. But this synagogue, built as a single-storey construction, could not accommodate such an addition, and therefore it was extended sideways.

Any male visitors to the synagogue should be aware that they are required to wear skull caps (*kippah*) before entering, out of respect. Paper caps are handed out at the entrance.

Starý židovský hřbitov

This cemetery was established in the 15th century when the Jewish people were not permitted to be buried anywhere other than in their own designated graveyard, therefore this relatively tiny space had to accommodate the burial plots of the entire community from 1439 until the last funeral in 1787. For this reason one grave was piled on top of another in a pitiably hotch-potch fashion as they did all they could to lay their loved ones to rest with some attempt at dignity. It is thought that there are around 12,000 graves here, with plots going down at least 12 layers, although in all probability there are hundreds more.

The oldest located tombstone dates from 1439 and marks the burial site of Avigdor Karo, noted poet of the age. The most famous grave, however, is that of Rabbi Löw, of Golem fame (1520–1609). Other important graves are those of Mayor Mordechai Maisel (1528–1601), Rabbi David Oppenheim (1664–1736), who is revered for his painstaking collection of valuable Hebrew manuscripts, and

Above left: The cemetery is called "Beth Chaim" or "House of Life"
Above right: Carved detail of an old gravestone in the cemetery

✚ **77 B2**

✉ **Starý židovský hřbitov**
Široká 3

☎ 221 711 511

WWW **www.jewishmuseum.cz**

🕐 Apr–Oct, Sun–Fri 9–6; Nov–Mar, Sun–Fri 9–4:30

💰 Expensive

🚇 Staroměstská

the Jewish astronomer David Gans
(1541–1613).

The majority of the burials were overseen
by the Prague Burial Society, whose role
it was to ensure that all Jewish funereal
rituals were followed despite the dire
conditions of the cemetery. One of the most
moving aspects of the whole site is the
Nephele Mound, a sorrowful plot that was
designated for infants.

Despite the cramped surroundings, the
Jewish community always treated death
with a great deal of respect and decorum
and, although crumbling today, many of the
tombstones are elaborately decorated with
symbols that either denote wishes for the
afterlife, or the profession or family name
of the deceased. A violin, for example,
indicates that the departed was a musician;
a pair of scissors, a tailor, and so on. More
important families, such as the Cohens,

had their own dynastic symbols that can be
seen repeated throughout the cemetery.

The cemetery is now looked after by
the extensive Jewish Museum of Prague,
and the graves area is cordoned off from
the pathways to avoid, if possible, any
further disintegration of the site. The place
is invariably crowded, but little can distract
from the moving atmosphere.

Above: Many headstones are crowded
in to a tiny space at the Jewish
Cemetery
Above right: The tomb of Chief Rabbi
Löw who died in 1609, set beneath
the trees of the Old Jewish Cemetery
Right: A gravestone depicting three fish
entwined with one another

Uměleckoprůmyslové muzeum

The most important collection within Prague's Museum of Decorative Arts is its Bohemian glassware. There is plenty of evidence that the Czechs were making top-quality glass products from the Middle Ages onwards, but it is really in the 17th century that their skills began to surpass rival nations, with engraved glass (an innovative technique) being exported to royal households and aristocracy throughout Europe.

In the early 19th century, coloured glass was experimented with and became extremely popular, either plain or engraved, as did mirrored glass. And, of course, in the early 20th century, Czechs produced some of Europe's finest art nouveau glass

products. Some of the most exquisite pieces produced in Bohemia between the 17th and 20th centuries are now on display in the museum, which also gives a detailed history of the industry and of the skills and techniques used. Among other exhibits are

ceramics, porcelain, carpets, tapestries, and a collection of furniture spanning various styles over the centuries. The art nouveau artist Alfons Mucha is widely represented through his commercial posters and photography, as are world-renowned photographers such as Man Ray. There's also a fascinating section devoted to fashion and textiles through the ages, from elaborate liturgical vestments to flamboyant 1920s flapper dresses.

Children, meanwhile, will enjoy the area devoted to the history of toy-making, from simple wooden items to the mechanical pieces of the 20th century.

Above left: Exterior of the Decorative Arts Museum, which houses the country's largest collection of arts and crafts

Above: An exquisite stained-glass composition on the stairs of the museum

✚ **77 B2**

✉ **Uměleckoprůmyslové muzeum**
17 listopadu 2

☎ 251 093 111

www.upm.cz

⏱ Tue 10–7, Wed–Sun 10–6

✋ Moderate

Ⓜ Staroměstská

Vysoká synagoga

The High Synagogue was once joined the adjacent Jewish Town Hall, but was given a separate entrance in the 19th century. Astonishingly, the Nazis hoped to open a museum of the extinct Jewish race once they had systematically wiped them out from Europe – their defeat, needless to say, scuppered any such horrific plans.

The High Synagogue was originally established by Mordechai Maisel, the influential Jewish Mayor of Prague in the 16th century. It was designed as a preaching place for councillors of the Jewish Town Hall. Near by is the Maiselova Synagogue named after him, which is still in the possession of the Jewish Museum.

In the Maiselova Synagogue you can visit the exhibition exploring the history of the Jewish community in Bohemia from first arrival to emancipation. It's a fascinating insight into the establishment of the ghetto, the lives lived within it over the centuries, and the rules and regulations that the Jewish community were forced to follow. Also on display are various precious silverwork items, Hebrew manuscripts, prayer shawls and other artefacts rescued from a number of synagogues in the region.

Inside the High Synagogue are rich Renaissance details and vaulted ceilings. Having served some time as part of the Jewish Museum, the building has been returned to its purpose as a working synagogue on the first floor and is closed to non-Jews, except for the small gift shop on the ground floor. In 1938 the number of synagogues in Prague was 360. This figure was reduced to 200, of which only three were working places of worship. Vysoká Synagogue was one of them. The others were used either as Christian churches, museums, cultural institutions, schools or storage. Some remained empty.

Left: The exterior of the Jewish Town Hall in the Josefov area. Vysoká Synagoga (High Synagogue), attached to the left of the building, was financed by Mayor Mordecai Maisel. The edifice is a mid-18th century rebuilding of an earlier structure with the Star of David on top of the belfry

✚ **77 B2**

✉ **Vysoká synagoga**
Červená 4

🕓 Closed to the public

🚇 Staroměstská

✉ **Maiselova synagoga**
Maiselova 10

☎ 221 711 511

🌐 **www.jewishmuseum.cz**

🕓 Apr–Oct, Sun–Fri 9:30–6; Nov–Mar, Sun–Fri 9:30–5

✋ Expensive

Židovská radnice

The first Jewish Town Hall dates, like so much in the Jewish Quarter, from the period in the 16th century when the wealthy Mayor Maisel did much to renovate the area. The current pink-and-white building seen is, however, a rococo creation added during renovation in the late 18th century. Today, the building operates, as it always did, as a community centre for the Jewish residents of Prague, and is officially known as the Federation of Jewish Communities in the Czech Lands.

This was the place where Jewish scholars were employed by the Nazis to collect material for a museum titled "Exotic Museum of an Extinct Race". One of its most notable features is its clock tower featuring two different clock faces. The top one follows standard Roman time and numerals; the lower clock features Hebrew figures, with the hands turning anti-clockwise in the Hebrew tradition.

The only section of the town hall currently open to non-Jews is the kosher restaurant, Shalom, on the ground floor, which is one of the most popular eateries in the city.

A little further along the street, on the corner of U Radnice, is a statue of Franz Kafka, one of the most famous Jewish people to have been born in Prague.

Left: Detail of the lower of the two clocks decorating the exterior of the Jewish Town Hall, going anti-clockwise, with Hebrew numerals
Above: The Old-New Synagogue with the Jewish Town Hall and clock tower on the right

✚ **77 B2**

✉ **Židovská radnice**
Maiselova 18

🌐 **www.upm.cz**

🚫 Closed to the public

🚇 Staroměstská

Malá Strana

The Malá Strana (Lower Quarter) is dominated by beautiful baroque houses that were once home to the aristocratic elite. In parts, the narrow streets and beautiful gardens lend it a sense of intimacy and serenity. Popular with artists and writers, it's an area of small craft shops and charming little cafés and bars, many of which lay out tables on the cobbled streets in good weather. It's also the gateway to Prague's main park, Petřínské sady, which, on a summer's day, offers one of the city's most relaxing excursions and wonderful views over the rooftops.

MALÁ STRANA WALK

1. Karlův most
See page 112

The Charles Bridge has long been an important route in Prague. Today it is usually the most crowded part of the city, as visitors flock here not only to admire the wonderful architecture but to join in the party atmosphere that the street entertainers create. Walk straight up Mostecká and turn right on to Tomášská.

2.Valdštejnský palác
See page 122

The Wallenstein Palace is a wonderful example of elaborate baroque architecture, both inside and out, although much of the interior is closed to the public. It is also set within beautiful landscaped gardens full of fountains and sculptures. Come down Tomášská and turn right on to Nerudova.

3. Nerudova
See page 116

This lovely street between the Little Quarter and the castle is notable for its elaborate house signs, which were used to identify residences before the system of house numbering came into place. Many of the larger and more impressive buildings are now home to embassies from around the world. Turn left on to Malostranské náměstí.

4. Chrám sv Mikuláše
See page 108

Prague's other Church of Saint Nicholas, not to be confused with the one in the Old Town, has an explosion of baroque splendour within its walls. The highlights of the building are the dome, stunningly painted with religious imagery, and the striking organ. Walk south down Karmelitská and turn left down Harantova towards the river.

5. Kampa Island
See page 110

This small "island" area makes for a wonderful peaceful stroll, amid tiny craft shops, old-style pubs and former mill houses. You can also rent a canoe if you feel like it, but mainly this is a quiet place for escaping the city crowd.

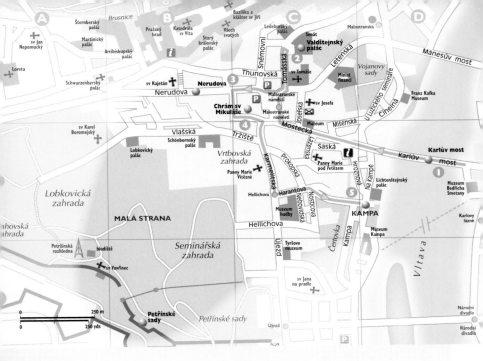

Chrám sv Mikuláše

Malá Strana's Church of St Nicholas is the crowning glory of baroque architecture in Prague. It was designed and built by Christoph Dientzenhofer and his even more talented son Kilián Ignaz Dientzenhofer, whose baroque contributions to the city landscape in the 18th century surpassed all others.

The exterior is typical of the period, featuring an expressive white façade topped with a huge dome and a bell tower dominating the landscape. Visitors can climb the bell tower for a wonderful panorama of the city – the views are so good, in fact, that it was used as a look-out post by the Secret Police during the Communist regime.

Inside, however, is the true masterpiece of the church – the central 70m (230-foot) high dome decorated with a stunning fresco entitled the *Celebration of the Holy Trinity*. The altar beneath is an example of high baroque flamboyance, with beautiful panel paintings. The marble pulpit, too, is splendid with its excellent gilt carvings

depicting angels, cherubs, flowers and plants. Above the main entrance is the vast organ that once had the privilege of being played by Mozart. A mural above depicts the life of St Cecilia, the patron saint of music. The life of the church's namesake, St Nicholas, is depicted in the beautiful ceiling fresco by Jan Lukáš Kracker. The Passion cycle of paintings is also a priceless addition to the church and is the work of Karel Škréta.

✚ **107 C1**

✉ **Chrám sv Mikuláše**
Malostranské náměstí

☎ 257 534 215

🌐 **www.psalterium.cz**

🕐 Mar–Oct, daily 9–5; Nov–Feb, 9–4

✋ Inexpensive

Ⓜ Malostranská

Above left: Front of St Nicholas's Church showing the symmetry in design
Above right: Figures of angels soar above the magnificent organ that Mozart played on

Kampa Island

Situated just beneath the Charles Bridge, Kampa Island is a lovely, peaceful enclave of the Lower Quarter formed by a small stream of water, known as Čertovka (Devil's Stream), flowing off from the Vltava. The water was turned to the city's advantage by allowing several flour mills to operate here – the water wheel of the Grand Priory Mill is still operational. During the 1960s the island was a favourite gathering spot for the city's hippies, who adorned the walls with brightly coloured murals.

The most favourite mural that still survives the hippy days is a portrait of former Beatle John Lennon. The area has been dubbed the "Venice of Prague" and the few houses here are the most sought after in the city.

The area is filled with greenery and park land and is one of the best places for escaping the crowds milling around the bridge above. There are a number of small restaurants and wine bars below Charles Bridge and Na Kampě, where souvenir shops abound, and some charming art galleries, as well as a children's playground.

Left and above: The cobbled paving of Kampa Square bordered by a row of apartment houses

✚ **107 D2**

✉ **Kampa Island**

Ⓜ Malostranská

Karlův most

Linking the Old Town with the Lower Quarter and Hradčany across the Vltava River, the 515m (1,690-foot) long Charles Bridge is one of the most popular sights in Prague.

An older stone bridge, known as Judith Bridge, straddled the water here since the 10th century, but it was destroyed in a flood. The current bridge, named after Charles IV who commissioned the structure, was begun in 1357 by the city's most prominent medieval architect Peter Parler. Originally, the bridge formed part of the Royal Route, when newly crowned kings would journey from the Old Town to the castle, but today the full length is entirely pedestrianised.

The highlight of the bridge, apart from the views it offers of each half of the city, are the statues that line its length, many of which have legends and stories attached to them. The oldest statue is of St John Nepomuk, erected in 1683. The medieval priest was murdered on the orders of

Above left: Looking down the Vltava at the bridges crossing it, Charles Bridge is in the centre
Above right: A view from the Bridge Tower of local traders and tourists strolling along Charles Bridge

✚ **107 D2**

✉ **Karlův most**

◷ Open access

Ⓜ Malostranská or Staromestská

Wenceslas IV, and his tortured body thrown off the bridge into the icy waters below. Touching the statue is said to bring good luck, which explains the various spots that are tarnished or seem to have worn away on the bronze reliefs.

The rest of the statues, the majority of which are copies of the originals, either depict biblical themes, such as the Pietà and the crucifixion, or canonised men and women who had played an important role in the history of the city. St Vitus is depicted befriending a pride of lions, the beautiful St Luitgard statue shows the visionary saint healing Christ's wounds, while Roland (or Bruncvík) honours the knight whose sword, believed to be buried within the bricks of the bridge, is said to protect Prague should the city ever be likely to fall. The statue of St Wenceslas was a 19th-century addition erected during the National Revival movement in honour of the city's patron saint.

At each end of the bridge are two wonderful Gothic towers that protected the entrance to the Old Town and the Lower Quarter respectively. The Old Town Bridge Tower has a viewing gallery at the top, which offers breathtaking views across the river and up to the castle.

The bridge has often played a vital role in history. The final battle of the brutal Thirty Years War was staged here, when the Czechs vanquished the invading Swedes, it was a link between the opposing sides during the revolutions of 1848. Today, however, the noise and bustle is due to an altogether more jovial atmosphere, as jazz buskers line the route and stallholders sell souvenirs to the throngs of tourists that come here every day.

Left: A statue of one of the female saints revered in the city on Charles Bridge
Above left: Looking across Charles Bridge with the Bridge Tower in the distance and the city buildings spreading out behind
Above right: A busker sitting under one of the statues

Nerudova

This steep street leading from the Lower Quarter to the castle district is best known for its house signs – a practice in Prague used to identify trades and residences before street numbering simplified the matter. (The tradition continues to live on here, as in Britain, with its pub and wine bar signs.) At the Two Suns (now No 47) is the former home of one of the Czech Republic's most revered writers, Jan Neruda, in whose honour the street is named because many of his stories were set in this area.

The most impressive buildings on the street are the former "palaces" of noble families, built in the 18th century in baroque style, the majority of which are now used as embassies for countries around the world, such as the Thun-Hohenštejnský palác at No 20, now the Italian Embassy. The façade of the Morzinský palác (Romanian Embassy) at No 5 is famous for its balcony, supported by statues of two Moors.

At No 32, the traditional 19th-century Dittrich Pharmacy has been preserved as a museum as part of the National Museum's collection, with a fascinating display of traditional cures and medical instruments.

Left: General view along Nerudova in the Malá Strana; the street forms the final stretch of the Royal Route
Above: Stamps in the window of No 51, Philately Antik, on Nerudova

✚ **107 B1**

✉ **Nerudova**

Dittrich Pharmacy

☎ 257 531 502

🌐 **www.nm.cz**

🕑 Tue–Sun 11–5 (closes at 6 Apr–Oct)

✋ Inexpensive

Ⓜ Malostranská

Petřínské sady

One of the loveliest places to go during any trip to Prague is up the hill to Petřín Park, once consisting of vineyards but now a collection of flower-filled (in spring and summer) gardens. It's a relatively steep walk so the best way to reach the park is via the funicular railway (Lanová dráha), originally dating from the 19th century, when it was operated by a complicated system of water and weights, but renovated in the 1980s and now powered by electricity. The park offers not only wonderful views of the city down below but has plenty of attractions in its own right.

The Observation Tower (Rozhledna) is the most distinctive sight, erected in 1891 as a replica of Paris's Eiffel Tower. If you want views far beyond the city boundaries you can climb to the top, but be warned – there's no lift, just 299 increasingly tiring steps.

Of particular interest to children is the Mirror Maze (Zrcadlové bludiště), housed in a fanciful pavilion, one of the many built in mock-Gothic style for the Jubilee Exhibition held in 1891. Confusing corridors are lined with trick mirrors that distort the body in all manner of shapes and sizes, a sight that induces hysterical laughter no matter how old or sensible you are. More seriously, there's also a popular diorama on display here that illustrates the battle between the Czechs and the Swedes on the Charles Bridge in 1648.

A slightly incongruous Russian-style building within the park is the older 17th-century Church of St Michael. It comes from the Ukraine, and was brought here in 1929 when its home village was briefly a part of Czechoslovakia. The interior is closed to the public, but its lovely wooden structure, pagoda roofs and onion domes are well worth a look.

Left: A stunning view of the church of St Lawrence in the lush green Kinsky Gardens on Petřín Hill

---

✚ **107 B3**

✉ **Petřínské sady**

🕐 Daily 5am–midnight

🚋 Tram 1, 2, 18

Observation Tower

☎ 257 320 112

🕐 Apr, daily 10–7; May–Jun and Sep, daily 10–10; Oct, daily 10–6; Nov–Mar, Sat–Sun 10–5

✋ Inexpensive

Mirror Maze

☎ 257 315 212

🕐 Apr and Sep, daily 10–7; May, daily 10–10; Oct, daily 10–6; Jun–Aug, daily 10–8; Nov–Mar, Sat–Sun 10–5

✋ Inexpensive

For star-gazers, Prague's Stefanick Observatory (Stefanikova hvězdárna; see www.observatory.cz for times; inexpensive) has high-spec telescopes looking out to the galaxy beyond. Scientists such as Tycho Brahe (1546–1601) have given Prague a historic link with astronomy and there's an exhibition detailing the discoveries over time.

The main wall within the park is known as the Hunger Wall (Hladová zed), because it was constructed by the city's starving population during a famine in the 14th century, on the orders of Charles IV to provide them with employment.

Far left: Exterior of the Mirror Maze, housed in a mock Gothic structure
Left: The Observation Tower on Petřín Hill built especially for the Jubilee Exhibition
Above: St Michael's church is an example of the timber construction of Ruthenia, a region attached to Czechoslovakia in 1919 and now part of Ukraine

Valdštejnský palác

The striking Wallenstein Palace, the first baroque building in Prague, is a cautionary reminder of over ambition. It was built in the 17th century by the vainglorious Albrecht von Wallenstein (1581–1634), who rose to become Commander of the Imperial Armies under the Habsburgs, whom he served in the Thirty Years War. He wanted his home to reflect his power and achievement under the ruler Ferdinand II. Sadly, he only had four years in which to enjoy it – his ambition got the better of him and when he attempted to seek the crown he was murdered by the same court that had enabled his success.

Above left: The Wallenstein Gardens, lined with copies of statues by Dutchman Adriaen de Vries
Above right: Relief work on a heavy brass door on the exterior of Wallenstein Palace

Today the magnificent building is owned by the Czech government and used for state occasions, but there are guided tours around parts of the palace on weekends. The gardens (Valdštejnská zahrada) that surround the building are readily accessible and the landscaped courtyards make for a lovely stroll.

Highlights include the flamboyant pavilion (*sala terrena*), a grotto of stalactites and its statuary, though these are replicas of the 17th-century originals. The gardens are particularly popular in summer when they are the setting for open-air classical music concerts. The palace also once had its own riding school, but the building is now occupied by part of the National Gallery, which stages temporary exhibitions here from time to time.

✚ **107 C1**

✉ **Valdštejnský palác**
Valdštejnské náměstí 4

☎ 257 071 111

▥ **www.senat.cz**

◑ Sat–Sun 10–4; Gardens Apr–Oct, daily 10–6

✋ Moderate

Ⓜ Malostranská

Nové Město

The "New Town" is a bit of a misnomer since the area dates from the 14th century and the rule of Holy Roman Emperor Charles IV. However, in comparison to the Old Town, established more than 300 years earlier, it was comparatively new. From its inception the area's focus has been trade and commerce, and it is still very much the commercial and business heart of Prague. Much of it was also redeveloped or expanded in the 19th century, so it has a wonderful array of buildings of the National Revival period and some stunning art nouveau façades.

NOVÉ MĚSTO WALK

1. Václavské náměstí
See page 138

History seems to run through the veins of almost every street in Prague. But it is largely 20th-century events that are evident on Wenceslas Square, evocatively captured in the Monument to the Victims of Communism. The long square is also a popular shopping and nightlife area. Start the walk at the southern end of the square.

2. Národní muzeum
See page 134

The National Museum of the Czech Republic is the main feature of the southern end of Wenceslas Square. Inside are rather dour collections dedicated to subjects such as natural history and archaeology, but it is worth visiting for the architecture alone. Continue two blocks north up the square.

3. Hotel Evropa
See page 128

One of Prague's most beautiful art nouveau buildings remains a draw for its elegant café with wonderful over-the-top mirrors and decorations. There's also a very popular outdoor café although this rather misses the point, without the architecture. Turn right on to Jindřišská and left on to Panská.

4. Muchovo muzeum
See page 130

The Mucha Museum is dedicated to the revered Alfons Mucha, probably the best-known artist to have emerged from the Czech art world. He is remembered for his theatrical posters and designs about the nascent Czechoslovak Republic. Walk to the top of Panská and turn left on to Na příkopě, continuing towards the river along Národní.

5. Národní divadlo
See page 132

Prague's National Theatre is a gem of neo-Renaissance architecture looking out over the Vltava River. Its intricacy owes itself to the optimism of the National Revival period in the last decades of the 19th century, and it makes a fine place to end your walk.

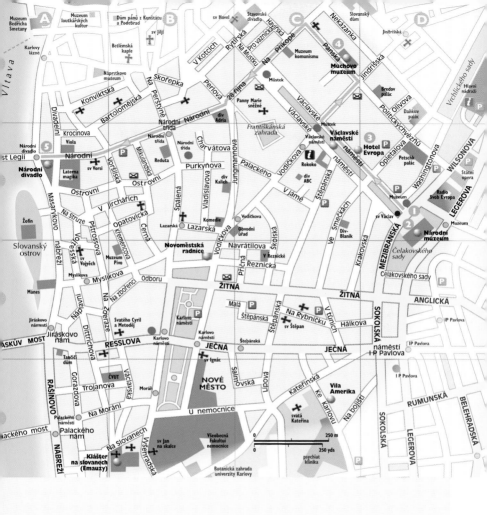

Hotel Evropa

The Europa Hotel, built between 1903 and 1906, is a landmark on the landscape of Wenceslas Square and is one of the finest examples of art nouveau hotels in the whole of Europe.

✚ **127 D2**

✉ **Hotel Evropa**
Václavské náměstí 25

☎ 224 215 387

www.evropahotel.cz

Ⓜ Můstek

The hotel's façade is dominated by the dome-shaped pediment adorned with gold statues, while inside, the Café Evropa and the Titanic restaurant are both beautifully preserved examples of the art nouveau style with their extravagant mirrors and gold fittings. Sadly, the rooms seem rather bland, and in some cases spartan, after all the grandness below. Some rooms have rather functional 1970s-style furniture, but staying here amid the sweeping staircase, balconies and chandeliers is still quite an experience.

Above: The yellow façade of the Hotel Evropa is a change from the white and green buildings so common in the city

Klášter na slovanech

The Slavonic Monastery (sometimes referred to as the Emmaus Monastery) dates from 1347 and was built for an order of Benedictine monks. It remains a working monastery, although the building has changed much over the centuries.

The biggest tragedy to befall the monastery was an air raid during World War II. So much of what is seen today is a 1960s re-creation, including the two modern spires. Fortunately a few of the 14th-century murals in the cloisters survived the disaster. The monastery's main claim to fame was its creation of exquisite illuminated manuscripts in the Slavonic language.

Above: Inside the renovated Slavonic Monastery

✚ **127 B4**

✉ **Klášter na slovanech**
Vyšehradská 49

☎ 221 979 211

🌐 **www.emauzy.cz**

🕓 Mon–Fri 9–4

✋ Inexpensive

🚇 Muzeum

Muchovo muzeum

Alfons Mucha (1860–1939) was one of Europe's greatest exponents art nouveau and this relatively new museum is dedicated to the Czech artist's work.

Set in a former aristocrat's house, the baroque building is crammed with Mucha masterpieces, including his most famous works depicting the great 19th-century French actress Sarah Bernhardt. His sketchbooks, in particular, offer a wonderful insight into the manner in which his distinctive style was created.

While Mucha's Parisian work is undoubtedly his most recognisable, the artist returned to Prague from France in 1910, drawn by the atmosphere of the National Revival movement and the steady progress towards Czech independence. Most of his work dating from this period included designing much of the interior of the Municipal House and a stained-glass window for St Vitus's Cathedral. He also produced his most comprehensive work, known as the *Slav Epic*, which attempted

MUCHA museum

OTEVÍRACÍ DOBA / OPENING HOURS
DENNĚ / DAILY 10 A.M. - 6 P.M.

to illustrate the history of the Slav people through imagery.

Returning to the Paris period, there's also a carefully reconstructed version of his French studio, with his painting materials, easel and family photographs on display. Those who want to know more about the man and his work can sit through a documentary, but this is really only for die-hard aficionados.

Above left: A fanciful baroque decoration on the façade of the building
Above right: A poster depicts Mucha's famous sketch of the legendary actress Sarah Berhardt

✚ **127 C1**

✉ **Muchovo muzeum**
Kaunický palác, Panská 7

☎ 224 216 415

www.mucha.cz

◑ Daily 10–6

✋ Moderate

Ⓜ Muzeum

Národní divadlo

The Czech National Theatre is one of the most important buildings in the country as far as the Czech people are concerned. This is largely because its construction was funded mostly by the people themselves by way of donations during the National Revival period.

Before it was built, there were only German theatres where Czech plays were sometimes performed. This original building was designed by Josef Zítek and opened with much fanfare in 1881 with a performance of *Libuše*, the opera by Bedřich Smetana, the "father" of Czech music. Tragically, however, the building was entirely ravaged by fire just two months later and had to be rebuilt from scratch; this time architect Josef Schulz was appointed to design the theatre and, two years later, the neo-Renaissance building seen today once more staged *Libuše* to mark its second opening. It remains one of the most striking buildings on the banks of the Vltava, adorned with statues depicting different aspects of the arts.

The building's highlight is its stunning auditorium, with a beautiful ceiling fresco from which hangs a magnificent chandelier and a gilded proscenium arch. There is also a sumptuous box reserved for the president (once meant for royalty) that depicts various figures who played a major role in the history of the country.

Next door to the theatre is the rather controversial Nová scéna, a futuristic glass structure that is somewhat at odds with the elegance of the National Theatre.

Above left: The grand building hosting fine performances
Above right: Inside the huge hall of the theatre

🔟 **127 A2**

✉ **Národní divadlo**
Národní 2

☎ 224 901 111

🌐 **www.narodni-divadlo.cz**

🕐 For performances only

✋ Moderate to expensive

🚇 Národní třida

Národní muzeum

The landmark at the southern end of Wenceslas Square is Prague's National Museum, set in an imposing 19th-century neo-Renaissance building by Josef Schulz, the same architect responsible for the rebuilt National Theatre. The interiors of the museum are breathtaking, especially the main staircase adorned with busts, columns and statues.

The main focus of the collections is history, including natural history. There are areas dedicated to palaeontology, geology, archaeology, anthropology and the prehistoric life found in Bohemia. As befits the oldest and most important museum in the country there's also a strong focus on national history, with a collection of folk art and textiles. It also tells the history of the arts in the Czech Republic, and includes some rare musical instruments, as well as weaponry, coins and medals. Temporary exhibitions are held throughout the year, often containing pieces that lack of space prevents from being displayed. The library contains priceless documents which chronicle various aspects of the country, its history and the people who shaped it. In another part of the museum, known as the Pantheon, is a splendid collection of busts celebrating the great and the good of Czech history.

✚ **127 D2**

✉ **Národní muzeum**
Václavské náměstí 68

☎ 224 497 111

🅦🅦🅦 **www.nm.cz**

🕓 May–Sep, daily 10–6; Oct–Apr, 9–5; closed first Tue of the month

✋ Moderate

🚇 Muzeum

Left: Exterior of the National Museum
Above: Detail of a sculpture depicting a mother and child

Novoměstská radnice

The New Town Hall, having first been built in the 14th century, then renovated 200 years later, is a blend of Gothic and Renaissance styles. It served as the Town Hall until the late 18th century, after which it was converted to a magisterial court and, conveniently, a prison. The most dominant feature of the building is its Gothic tower. Today its purpose is largely ceremonial and several portions of the building are closed to the public. There is a small art gallery inside that's worth a look.

Above left: The tower of the reconstructed New Town Hall, historically the site of the first defenestration
Above right: A sculptured head in the garden of the New Town Hall

The most important moment in the building's history came in 1419 when the Hussite leader Jan Želivský and his men stormed the building in protest at several of their followers being held prisoner. When the town councillors refused to release them, the mob attacked and threw them out of the window. Most were fatally injured in the fall; those who survived were beaten to death by the violent mob outside. In what was to become known as the first defenestration of Prague, it marked the beginning of the Hussite Wars that were to last several decades. The statue that now stands in front of the New Town Hall is of Ževliský, erected in 1960 in honour of his deeds for the Czech people.

✚ **127 B3**

✉ **Novoměstská radnice**
Karlovo náměstí 23

☎ 224 948 229

🌐 **www.novomestskaradnice.cz**

🕐 May–Sep, Tue–Sun 10–6

✋ Inexpensive

🚇 Karlovo náměstí

Václavské náměstí

The most important street in the New Town area is Wenceslas Square, stretching some 750m (2,460 feet). In the Middle Ages there used to be a horse market here, and commerce is still its main focus, with its many shops, several of which are housed in arcades, restaurants and cinemas.

✚ **127 C2**

✉ **Václavské náměstí**

🚇 Můstek or Muzeum

The area of most interest is at the southern end of the square, marked by the façade of the National Museum. In front of this is a statue of St Wenceslas on horseback, flanked by other Czech patron saints. Wenceslas is best known the world over for the Christmas Carol "Good King Wenceslas", although much of the 19th-century lyrics are anachronistic to the real history. Nevertheless, the duke (and not king), who was murdered by his

Above: The Jan Palach memorial attracts patriotic Czechs even today
Right: Number 34 or Wiehl House, a good example of the art nouveau style

jealous brother Boleslav in AD 935, is still much revered in the country, partly for his promotion of Christianity and partly because legend has now become in some way truth.

The statue was erected in 1912 at a time when the country was heading towards independence and was thus celebrating its proud past. This area has long been a political gathering place in a nation that has seen its fair share of political strife. Jubiliations of independence were held here in 1918; in 1939 this is where Hitler made his own proclamations. This was also where protestors gathered to oppose the Soviet invasion in 1968, known as the Prague Spring, and where, in 1969, the world watched in horror as a student named Jan Palach set himself on fire in opposition to the new rule.

On a happier note, crowds gathered at Wenceslas Square to celebrate the downfall of the Communist regime following the 1989 Velvet Revolution. In front of the statue, usually surrounded by flowers and bouquets, is the Monument to Victims of Communism (Obětem komunismu), which honours Palach and many others who suffered at the hands of the oppressive government.

Moving down the "square" (actually a long straight road) there are many examples of Prague's love for the art nouveau style, such as the Hotel Evropa and Wiehl House, whose façade is adorned with art nouveau murals. A little further down is the Franciscan Garden (Františkánská zahrada), a lovely public garden in an otherwise quite urban setting that once belonged to a monastery, hence its name.

At the end of the square is the Church of Our Lady of the Snows (Kostel Panny Marie Sněžné), built in the 14th century at the request of Charles IV. The church is the burial place for the Hussite leader Jan Želviský. At the end of the street is the Koruna Palace, now occupied by shops and offices but instantly recognisable by its crown at the top of the building.

Below: An equestrian statue of St Wenceslas stands in Wenceslas Square
Right: Wenceslas astride his horse on top of the Wenceslas Monument

VÉVODO · ČESKÉ · ZEMĚ · KNÍŽE · NÁŠ

Vila Amerika (Muzeum Antonína Dvořáka)

This lovely baroque house built by Kilián Ignaz Dientzenhofer, who was responsible for the two churches of St Nicholas, is now home to a museum dedicated to the life and works of one of the Czech Republic's greatest composers, Antonín Dvořák (1841–1904). Despite living in Great Britain and the United States, he never lost sight of his Czech roots, and his finest works such as *Slavonic Dances* and *From the New World* pay homage to his national identity.

While Bedrich Smetana may well be the number one favourite in the Czech musical pantheon, Dvořák comes a very close second. Numerous personal mementoes and effects of the composer are now on display in the museum, including his piano, the desk on which he wrote his scores, and many of the original scores themselves, all accompanied by taped music to enhance the atmosphere. The museum also often stages concerts of Dvořák's music.

Although the house was originally known as the Michna Summer Palace, after the family for which it was built, its current name comes from a nearby popular bar. In addition to the beautiful house and its collection there are lovely gardens to wander around.

Left: An ornate gateway frames part of the façade of the former summer villa, built between 1717 and 1720
Above: The ceiling fresco of the concert room is *Apollo, Pegasus and the Arts* by Johan Ferdinand Schor

✚ **127 C4**

✉ **Vila Amerika (Muzeum Antonína Dvoráka)**
Ke Karlovu 20

☎ 224 918 013

🖥 **www.nm.cz**

🕓 Apr–Sep, Tue–Sun 10–1, 2–5:30; Oct–Mar, Tue–Sun 9:30–1:30, 2–5

✋ Inexpensive

Ⓜ I P Pavlova

Further Afield

With so much to see and do in central Prague it may not seem necessary or viable to venture beyond the five main districts, particularly if you're only on a short weekend break. If you do have the time, however, there are plenty of attractions on the outskirts that are still readily accessible on the excellent metro network.

At the top of the list should be the mystical area of Vyšehrad, with its wonderful views and fascinating National Cemetery, while art-lovers can see one of the country's best collections of post 19th-century art in the Veletržní palác. For a taste of more day-to-day life away from the baroque quaintness of the city centre, head to the district of Žižkov, whose run-down streets are now experiencing a bit of an urban renewal.

Bertramka

Named after Frantisek Bertram, its second owner, this charming villa is where Wolfgang Amadeus Mozart (1756–91) and his friends the Duseks lived. It is now a museum dedicated to Mozart.

✉ **Bertramka**
Mozartova 169, Smíchov

☎ 257 317 465

🔳 **www.bertramka.com**

🕐 Apr–Oct, daily 9–6;
Nov–Mar, 9:30–4

✋ Moderate

🚇 Anděl

The great composer spent much of his time performing in Europe's capital cities and Prague was no exception. This house, where he lived for four years, celebrates his life in the Czech capital and the work he produced here, including parts of one of his finest operas, *Don Giovanni*, which premiered at the Estates Theatre in the Old Town. Another work, *La Clemenza di Tito,* was composed specifically for the coronation of Leopold II.

The house itself is a fine example of an 18th-century country villa and inside are numerous documents and pieces of memorabilia relating to the composer and his time in the house. From April to October the house is the venue for concerts of Mozart's music.

Above: A tree shades the cobbled square off which staircases lead to the covered veranda of Vila Bertramka; Mozart was supposedly locked up in a room while completing an aria here for Josefa Duskova

Letenské sady

One of the most popular areas locals visit to escape the city bustle is Letná Park, looking down over the Vltava River and the urban centre from a plateau in the northeast. This park once had the dubious fame of having the largest statue of Josef Stalin, erected in 1955, ten years after the Soviets first marched into the city and two years after the dictator's death.

The Czechs always hated this monument to the tyrannical leader and it was finally demolished with much drama in 1962. Today in its place is a rather incongruous metronome, that seems to keep time for nothing in particular. Meanwhile, the base of the original statue is generally crowded in good weather by teenage boys and girls practising their skateboarding skills. Another highlight of the park is the Hanavský Pavilion, built as a fanciful interpretation of the baroque style in 1891, which now houses a restaurant and café beneath its impressive dome.

Above: Sightseers looking towards the Old Town

✉ **Letenské sady**
Nábreží Edvarda Beneše, Letná

✋ Free

🚇 Malostranská or Hradčanská

147

Trojský zámek

During the 17th and 18th centuries, a trend emerged for Prague's noble families to build summer palaces outside of the city centre. The Troja Palace is one of the finest examples of these. It was completed in 1685 as a summer home for Count Sternberg in Italianate style, while the stunning landscaped gardens, complete with ornate fountains and sculpture emulate the French traditions that had become so famous at the Palace of Versailles. Within the grounds are an orangery, a maze and a small open-air theatre.

The house is reached by a wonderful two-tier staircase adorned with statues of gods and allegorical figures leading into its most striking feature, the Grand Hall. The frescoes may be a little sycophantic in their theme – glorifying the Habsburg Empire – but are sublime nonetheless.

Today some of the rooms are used as exhibition spaces for various art collections, such as furniture, ceramics and other chinoiserie in the Chinese Rooms and a collection of 19th-century Czech art in the Picture Gallery. There's also an exhibition entitled *Eternal Summer in the Roman Villa* that documents the construction of the palace, while in the former cellars there's an exhibition on the history of Czech wine-making, with tastings and sales.

Left: Statues decorate the staircase at the entrance to Troja Château
Above: A view through the of the château

✉ **Trojský zámek**
U Trojského zámku 1, Troja

☎ 283 851 614

🔲 **www.ghmp.cz**

🕐 Apr–Oct, Tue–Sun 10–6; Nov–Mar, Sat–Sun 10–5

✋ Moderate

🚇 Nádraží holešovice, then bus 112 to Zoologická zahrada

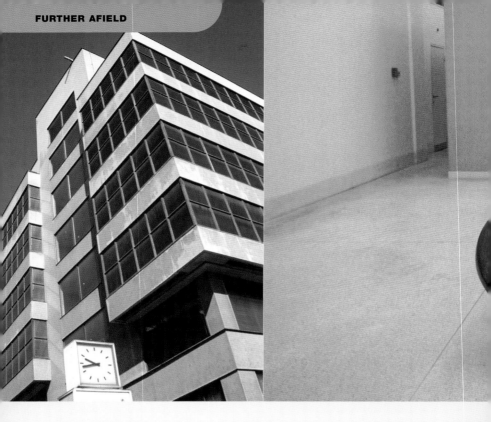

Veletržní palác

Known in English as the Trade Fair Palace (trade fairs were held here until the 1950s), this rather ugly building on the outskirts of Prague should not be missed for the treasures that it holds inside. Much of the National Gallery's collection of 19th- and 20th-century European art that was formerly on display in the Sternberg Palace moved here in 2000, because it offered far more scope for the great number of works to be on permanent exhibition. Exhibits from the modern period, however, that continue to expand into the 21st century, have been on display since the 1990s.

While there is an understandable emphasis on Czech art of the period, for most visiting art lovers the highlights are works by the French Impressionists and other European masters. Renoir, Manet, Cézanne, Degas, Rousseau, Dufy and Seurat are all

represented, as are Van Gogh and Chagall. There's also a striking self-portrait by Picasso dating from 1907. Other distinctive artists of the 20th century include Gustav Klimt and Egon Schiele. One of the loveliest paintings ever produced depicting Prague itself is *Charles Bridge and Hradčany* by the Austrian artist Oskar Kokoschka (1935).

Above left: The Trade Fair Palace houses the national collections of 19th-, 20th- and 21st-century art; it was completed in 1928, designed by the architects Oldřich Tyl and Josef Fuchs
Above right: *Motorcyclist (sunbeam)* by Otakar Sveč (1892–1955), an example of early 20th-century Czech art

✉ **Veletržní palác**
Dukelských hrdinů 47,
Holešovice

☎ 224 301 111

🌐 **www.ngprague.cz**

🕐 Tue–Sun 10–6 (first Wed of the month 10–8)

✋ Moderate, free first Wed of the month 3–8

Ⓜ Vltavská

Vyšehrad

This small suburb to the south of the city centre is steeped in legend and is thought to be the spot where Libuše, immortalised in Smetana's opera of the same name, began the Přemyslid dynasty that was to rule Prague for centuries from around AD 800. The rocky landscape made it an invaluable place for a fortress, given its defensive position. The remains of the castle, which continued to be important right into the Middle Ages, can still be seen. Much of the area now, however, is made up of tranquil parkland, dotted in places by statuary, including one commemorating Libuše herself.

The most striking building in Vyšehrad is the Church of St Peter and St Paul, with its neo-Gothic spires that emulate the original Gothic structure of the 14th century. But the largest attraction in the area is Vyšehrad cemetery, an area of land that was specifically set aside as a National Cemetery in the 19th century as the last resting place for those who had contributed to Czech history and culture. Among those buried here are the composers Bedřich Smetana and Antonín Dvořák, poets Jan Neruda, Karel Hynek Mácha and Karel Čapek, and art nouveau artist Alfons Mucha.

The other great attraction of any visit to Vyšehrad are the views its offers from its cliff-top position down to the rooftops of Prague's Old Town and the Vltava River.

Left: View of the River Vltava and Vyšehrad, with the Church of St Peter and St Paul visible
Above: Looking across Vyšehrad Cemetery you can see the spires of the Church of St Peter and St Paul

✉ **Vyšehrad**
South of the city centre

🌐 **www.praha-vysehrad.cz**

Ⓜ Vyšehrad

Žižkov

Today Žižkov is probably Prague's most multi-ethnic and bohemian (in the avant-garde sense) area, but it's also an important district in terms of the city's history.

Žižkov is named after the 15th-century Hussite leader Jan Žižka, who successfully defeated the Crusaders here in 1420. If there was any doubt as to how important the Czechs regard this hero, you only have to take a look at the statue of him astride his steed looking down from his hilltop position. The 10m (33-foot) high monument is considered to be the largest equestrian statue in the world. Behind him is the National Monument that has had a sadly chequered history. Initially built in 1929 to commemorate the struggles that the Czech people had endured to achieve independence, within just a few years it was commandered by the occupying Nazis and was even used as a burial site for Communist leaders, including Klement

Gottwald. It has thereby lost some of its original significance, but as it's a singularly unattractive structure, no one seems to be too concerned these days.

The other unavoidable and also controversial landmark of Žižkov is the 216m (709-foot) high Television Tower. Apart from being considered a blot on the landscape, other controversial matters arose during its construction – a former Jewish cemetery had to be desecrated to make way for it, and many believed that its was also a secret transmitter for the Communists against the West. It has a restaurant and an observation platform with great views.

Above left: View of the houses in the Žižkov district
Above right: A statue of Jan Žižka

✉ **Žižkov**

🚇 Jiřího z Poděbrad

Televizni vysilac (Television Tower)

☎ 242 418 778

🌐 **www.tower.cz**

🕐 Daily 10–11:30

✋ Moderate

Listings

The choice of where to eat, sleep, shop and party in Prague is so extensive that the following listings are only the tip of the iceberg. However, they have been selected to cover most budgets and areas of interest. Hotels range from jaw-droppingly grand to basic hostel-style accommodation, but there are a number of mid-range places which are both centrally located and beautiful. In recent years almost every world cuisine has found its way to Prague, but the list of restaurants here focuses largely on Czech cuisine. On your walks through the Old Town and around the castle, take a closer look at the charming gift and Bohemian glass shops that abound. For entertainment there's a never-ending calendar of things to do to suit all tastes – a Prague evening can be as quiet or as lively as you want it to be.

Accommodation

The range of hotel accommodation in Prague is vast, given the influx of tourists since the collapse of the Communist regime. Everything is on offer, from top-of-the-range international hotel chains, and charming boutique-style places set in former baroque palaces, to budget options (generally on the city outskirts) that lack architectural or stylistic imagination but are perfectly adequate places to stay. The popularity of the city, however, particularly as a weekend getaway during spring and summer, means that booking ahead is essential. If you arrive in Prague without pre-planned accommodation between April and October you are liable to be left out in the cold.

Staying in the centre of town is, of course, the ideal option – not only will all the sights be within walking distance, with ever more lanes and alleyways to explore en route, but the hotels, while generally either grand or charming in their own right, tend to be expensive. If you are looking for relatively inexpensive places to stay, however, suburbs such as Žižkov are a good bet – the Prague metro system is fast and reliable and you'll only spend 30 minutes or so each day getting to and from the centre. There are also a number of hostels available for the budget traveller, since staying in private apartments not only saves money but also offers a chance to engage with locals during your stay (try www.prague-hostels.cz or www.stopin.cz).

While travel agencies and tourist offices can help with booking accommodation, there are a number of online agencies from which to choose. The internet is a good bet because in such a competitive market you can find various discounts as long as you book well in advance.

Among the many agencies are www.pragueholiday.cz, www.pragueagency.com and www.accom-prague.cz – the list is virtually endless.

One of the reliable kiosks at the main railway station is that of the Prague Information Service (PIS), the official city information agency, who can also arrange accommodation at its other information offices. PIS also offer on-line reservation through its accommodation agency Pragotur (email: pragotur@pis.cz; tel: 221 714 130).

Prices listed for the following hotels are based on a double room with two people sharing during high season (April to October, and the Christmas and New Year period):

K under Kč2,000
KK Kč2,000–4,000
KKK over Kč4,000

STARÉ MĚSTO

Bellagio Hotel KKK
A recent addition to the Prague accommodation folio is this beautifully decorated, Italian-style 4-star hotel. Its Old Town location couldn't be more convenient.
✉ U milosrdných 2
☎ 221 778 999
🌐 www.bellagiohotel.cz

Betlem Club KK
Overlooking the historic Bethlehem Chapel this is a convenient location for all the sights but in a slightly quieter atmosphere than a lot of other central hotels. The 21 rooms are simple but stylishly decorated with wooden furniture, panelling and beams and there's a lovely Gothic-cellar dining area.
✉ Betlémské náměstí 9
☎ 222 221 574
🌐 www.betlemclub.cz

Cloister Inn KK
Not much character, but plenty of rooms (75) if you are in desperate need of a cheap place. If you want a place to rest your tired feet, the price and closeness to the National Theatre and the Bethlehem Chapel make it a good choice. Book in advance.
✉ Konviktská 14
☎ 224 211 020
🌐 www.cloister-inn.com

Four Seasons Hotel Prague KKK
Who can resist this member of the well-known luxury hotel chain. Its coveted site near the historic Charles Bridge gives it added attraction.
✉ Veleslavínova 2a
☎ 221 427 000
🌐 www.fourseasons.com/prague

Grand Hotel Praha KKK
A convenient location in the heart of the Old Town, with unbeatable views of the Astronomical Clock. The building itself is beautiful, set in a former baroque house. Rooms are decorated with antiques but include modern conveniences such as internet facilities.
✉ Staroměstské náměstí 22
☎ 222 369 521
🌐 www.hotels-of-prague.com

Hotel Antík KK
Another well situated hotel, minutes from the Old Town Square but set in one of the quieter streets, which makes for a more restful night. Formerly a 15th-century nobleman's house, its 12 rooms means it could probably qualify for boutique status and it certainly pays attention to most details. There's also a lovely patio garden.
✉ Dlouhá 22
☎ 222 322 288
🌐 www.antikhotels.com

Hotel Černý Slon KK
Only seconds from the Old Town Square, the Černý Slon (the name means Black

Elephant) is a 14th-century Gothic building that is now protected as an architectural treasure by UNESCO. The staff are friendly and helpful, and some rooms have internet access. There's also a pleasant wine bar in the cellar basement.

✉ Týnská 1
☎ 222 321 521
🌐 www.hotelcernyslon.cz

Hotel Pařiž KKK

In business since 1904 and still run by the original family, the beautiful Pařiž Hotel is an art nouveau gem minutes away from the Old Town Square and next door to the Municipal House. If you can afford it, this is one of the city's best places to stay.

✉ U Obecního domu 1
☎ 222 195 195
🌐 www.hotel-pariz.cz

Hotel Salvator KK

A relatively small (30-room) 3-star hotel with a warm welcoming atmosphere, a lovely restaurant and outdoor dining in summer. Rooms are light and airy, while the cellar basement, complete with a billiards table, is charming.

✉ Truhlářská 10
☎ 222 312 234
🌐 www.salvator.cz

Hotel Ungelt KKK

Something of a stalwart on Prague's accommodation scene, Hotel Ungelt offers 10 beautiful apartment-style rooms just minutes from the Old Town Square. Rooms are decorated in traditional style and there's a honeymoon suite, complete with pink chandelier. Price includes breakfast.

✉ Mala Stupartská 1
☎ 224 828 686
🌐 www.ungelt.cz

Intercontinental KKK

Opulence and shine were not quite in tune with Prague's more modest – though classic – aesthetics when this hotel opened in the 1970s. Massive by Prague standards, it has 364 rooms, but antique decorations give character to what could have been just another 5-star hotel.

✉ Rybná 20
☎ 221 700 111
🌐 www.prague.intercontinental.com

Josef KKK

The 5-star Josef offers every predictable luxury and there's plenty of choice between the 110 rooms if you book early enough. Definitely the place to be if you want to be pampered.

✉ Rýbná 20
☎ 221 700 111
🌐 www.hoteljosef.com

Tara K

Keep in mind there is no elevator and you will have to climb to the third and fourth floors, and then be squeezed into a tiny room. However, this 8-room pension is very reasonably priced and is especially suitable for backpackers, who would rather spend their day touring the city and using the accommodation just for crashing out at night.

✉ Havelská 15
☎ 224 228 083
🌐 www.pensiontara.net

U Krale Jiriho KK

King George's hotel has a pub conveniently located on its ground floor. This may be an attraction for some, but the rooms are comfortable too.

✉ Liliová 10
☎ 221 466 100
🌐 www.kinggeorge.cz

U Lilie KK

A very traditional, family-run bed and breakfast in the heart of the Old Town and very close to Charles Bridge. Upstairs are 17 comfortably appointed if slightly sparse rooms; downstairs a cosy restaurant serves hearty Czech fare.

✉ Liliová 15
☎ 222 220 432
ww www.pensionulilie.cz

U Medvídků KK

Upstairs in one of Prague's most famous beer houses are 33 charming attic-style rooms with beamed ceilings, wooden floors and a truly romantic atmosphere. What's more, all the sights are within easy walking distance and you can end your day with a refreshing glass of Budweiser in the medieval bar.

✉ Na Perštýně 7
☎ 224 211 916
ww www.umedvidku.cz

HRADČANY

Hotel Neruda KKK

About as close to the castle (100m/110yds) as you can get and set in a 14th- century converted convent on historic Nerudova. The rooms, are beautifully designed in contemporary style.

✉ Nerudova 44
☎ 257 535 557
ww www.hotel-neruda.com

Hotel U Brány KKK

This hotel, dating from the 15thcentury, is only a stone's throw from the gates of the castle. There are only 10 apartment-style rooms, so it books up fast. There's a popular restaurant on site, but more atmospheric is the cellar wine bar, where snacks are also available.

✉ Nerudova 21
☎ 257 534 050
ww www.ubrany.cz

Markéta K

Close to Prague Castle, this charming 26-room hotel is well worth the price. You can absorb some of the city's atmosphere by wandering around its quiet, tree-filled neighbourhood.

✉ Na Petynce 45, Břevnov

☎ 220 518 316
ww www.europehotels.cz

Romantik Hotel U Raka KKK

Within the lovely setting of Nový svět and just minutes from the castle, this charming hotel lives up to its romantic title. It offers a little touch of the countryside in the heart of the city centre, with its open fires, wooden beams and a lovely garden filled with potted plants.

✉ Černínská 10
☎ 220 511 100
ww www.romantikhotel-uraka.cz

U Krale Karla KK

The uphill walk from the tram stop is well worth it as you have the first glimpse of the historic King Charles' Hotel, which is comfortable and atmospheric. Further on, steps lead to Hradčany Square.

✉ Úvoz 4
☎ 257 5333 5949
ww www.romantikhotels.cz

JOSEFOV

Hotel President KKK

The 5-star President is one of the more popular hotels in Prague, just a few minutes' walk of the sights of the Jewish Quarter and the Old Town. Its décor seems a little dated these days, but there's a piano bar and the restaurant has great views of the river.

✉ Náměstí curieových 100
☎ 234 614 111
ww www.hotelpresident.cz

Maximilian KK

The Jewish Quarter is not the best hotel district of Prague, but this is a popular place, noted for its art nouveau décor, combined with contemporary attention to detail that has earned it praise from some of the most respected hotel critics.

✉ Haštalská 14
☎ 225 303 111
ww www.maximilianhotel.com

MALÁ STRANA

Aria Hotel KKK

Each floor of the charming Aria Hotel is dedicated to a different genre of music – classical, jazz, opera and pop, and each room in turn is dedicated to a renowned musician, from Elvis Presley to Luciano Pavarotti. It's one of the newest boutique hotels in Prague offering all the facilities of a 5-star hotel.

✉ Tržiště 9
☎ 225 334 111
⚏ www.aria.net

The Charles Bridge Residence KK

This truly elegant option right in the centre of town just steps away from the Charles Bridge. The baroque building has retained its historic style and all the guest rooms are decorated with replica furniture of the period, some also boasting ceiling frescoes or stained-glass windows.

✉ Mostecka 12
☎ 257 532 626
⚏ www.charlesbridgeresidence.com

Hotel U Zlaté Studně KKK

There's certainly an illustrious past to this building, whose name means "At the Golden Well" – both Emperor Rudolf II and the astronomer Tycho Brahe spent time in residence here in the 16th century. Renovated in the 1990s, it is now a wonderfully tranquil and elegant place to stay, tucked away in a lovely part of the Lower Quarter.

✉ U Zlaté Studně 4
☎ 257 011 213
⚏ www.goldenwellhotel.com

Mandarin Oriental KKK

The Mandarin Oriental is a somewhat incongruous name for a hotel that was once a monastery. The building's history goes back to the 1300s, as does that of the adjoining building, where the spa offers all kinds of exotic treatments.

✉ Nebovidská 1
☎ 233 088 888
⚏ www.mandarinoriental.com

Residence Lundborg KK

Almost all the accommodation in this lovely 4-star hotel have views of the Charles Bridge and the castle rising above it. Rooms range from hotel suites to apartment-style lodgings, some boasting original beamed ceilings.

✉ U Lužického semináře 3
☎ 257 011 911
⚏ www.lundborg.cz

Sax KK

If you want to stay in a quiet, restful place, then Sax is a good option. Its 22 rooms offer great views of the stylish Malá Strana district. They are comfortable and the staff are friendly and helpful.

✉ Janský vršek 3
☎ 257 531 268
⚏ www.sax.cz

NOVÉ MĚSTO

Adria Hotel KKK

Set directly on the great thoroughfare of Wenceslas Square, beside the Franciscan Gardens, this 4-star hotel has modern facilities within a historical building, as well as a convenient location.

✉ Václavské náměstí 26
☎ 221 081 111
⚏ www.adria.cz

Hotel Evropa K

This is probably the best-known hotel in Prague because of the striking art nouveau façade and its grand café. The rooms are a bit of a let-down, but you are staying in a piece of history and its location right on Wenceslas Square can't be beaten. It's also good value for money in this central area.

✉ Václavské náměstí 25
☎ 224 215 387
⚏ www.evropahotel.cz

Hotel Palace Praha KKK

The stunning 5-star Palace Praha in the heart of the New Town is a byword for luxury, with its canopied beds, marble bathrooms, a top-class restaurant and exclusive Gourmet Club.

✉ Panská 12
☎ 224 093 111
ｗ www.palacehotel.cz

Hotel 16 – U Sv Kateřiny KK

Just a few minutes' walk from Wenceslas Square you'll find this comfortable, no-frills hotel, which makes an ideal base for exploring the city. This lively area is particularly popular with night owls.

✉ Kateřinská 16
☎ 224 920 636
ｗ www.hotel16.cz

Hotel Yasmin KKK

Prague is turning its attentions increasingly to design-led hotels and the Hotel Yasmin is one of the newest of its kind. Only moments from Wenceslas Square and all the attractions and amenities that it affords, the Yasmin caters well for the business traveller, with conference facilities and in-room internet access, but the gym and sauna and a lovely terrace will appeal to all visitors.

✉ Politických vězňů 12
☎ 234 100 100
ｗ www.hotel-yasmin.cz

K&K Central KKK

The stylish, art nouveau K & K Central offers luxury at a price. Rooms are well-equipped and attractive and the location is excellent, just a few stops from the Municipal House. The group has another hotel, the Fenix, just off Wenceslas Square, another architectural landmark in art deco style and a good option for a stay in this delightful city.

✉ Hybernská 10
☎ 225 022 000
ｗ www.kkhotels.com

Salvator K

Another centrally placed hotel, near the Municipal House, the Salvator has a lovely central courtyard on to which some of the 32 rooms open out, creating a friendly atmosphere where guests can interact. A member of staff is always readily available.

✉ Trulářska 10
☎ 222 312 234
ｗ www.salvator.cz

FURTHER AFIELD

Ametyst KK

The Ametyst, just outside the centre, has earned itself the nickname of the 'Gallery Hotel' due to its constantly changing exhibitions of modern art by local artists. A chic, yet friendly 4-star hotel, it has stylish and well-equipped rooms.

✉ Jana Masaryka 11, Vinohrady
☎ 222 921 921
ｗ www.hotelametyst.cz

Hotel U Šemíka K

A peaceful 3-star hotel in the historic district of Vyšehrad, with wonderful views of the city. There's an on-site garden for summer evenings and a cosy fire in winter. Apartment accommodation is also available. The rooms are a little dated, but it's less expensive than staying in the heart of the city.

✉ Vratislavova 36, Vyšehrad
☎ 224 920 736
ｗ www.usemika.cz

Restaurants

The enormous impact of both tourists and expat residents in Prague has meant that the culinary scene in recent years has become almost unrecognisable from its former Communist days. Today you can experience fine dining every night of the week, tuck into fast-food from around the globe – be it pizza, curry or sushi – or enjoy traditional Czech dishes that have been the mainstay of the local menu for centuries. The restaurants, too, are as varied as the food – converted baroque palaces, summer terraces with astounding views, cosy cellar bars with Gothic vaulted ceilings.

For the most authentic experience, however, don't overlook traditional Czech venues. The local cuisine is hearty, to say the least, developed over the years to both stave off the winter cold and utilise locally grown ingredients. The emphasis is very much on meat – vegetarians will have a bland dining experience in this city – with pork, game and duck being the mainstays. These are often served with sweet sauces such as a plum gravy, and are invariably accompanied with a great deal of starch, in the form of bread or dumplings. Sauerkraut (pickled cabbage) is another ingredient that makes its way on to most plates.

Soups are the most popular form of starters, while pancakes or pastries such as strudel either round off a meal or provide an afternoon snack. These Czech eateries are homely – the service is generally very casual, and the wooden tables rarely have a tablecloth – but that's all part of the experience. There are plenty of designer-led restaurants, all chrome and glass, if you prefer to dine in modern, rather than traditional, surroundings.

Beer is the national drink in the Czech Republic, dominated by the Pilsner Urquell, Budvar, Staropramen and Gambrinus breweries, so you'll find a pub almost everywhere you turn. Many of these also serve snacks such as baked potatoes, a plate of cheese or a bowl of rich, steaming goulash.

Cafés here (known as *kavárna*), often displaying their original art nouveau décor, can make you feel as if you've stepped back into 1930s high society as you sip your coffee or tea and enjoy a selection of impossibly sweet cakes and pastries. Even if you don't usually stop for an afternoon break, try this traditional custom in Prague. For eating on the move, which is a likely event, the most traditional snacks are hot frankfurters or grilled sausage served with mustard. Stalls selling these local favourites can be found all over the city.

Eating out in Prague is a casual affair and you don't need to dress to impress in any but the most upmarket restaurants. Tips are expected by the staff – as a basic guideline round your bill up to the nearest 10 crowns.

Most restaurants open all day from 10am or noon to 10pm or 11pm. Lunch is generally served from noon to 3pm, and dinner from 6pm to 9pm. Cafés are usually open from 8am.

The price categories that are given are for a three-course meal for one person, excluding drinks:

K under Kč250
KK Kč250–700
KKK over Kč700

STARÉ MĚSTO

Allegro KKK
The riverside restaurant of the prestigious Four Seasons Hotel has been voted the country's best for its Bohemian specialities and cosmopolitan cuisine.
✉ Veleslavínova 2a
☎ 221 427 000

Amici Miei KKK
Straddling the area between the Old and the New Towns, this is one of the city's most highly regarded Italian restaurants. The veal escalopes are superb.
✉ Vězeňská 5
☎ 224 816 688

Au Gourmand Café K
Here you'll find freshly cooked sweet and savoury treats in a beautifully restored art noveau butcher's shop.
✉ Dlouhá 10
☎ 222 312 694

Barock KK
Trendy bar-restaurant well located on Prague's glitziest shopping street. Shop till you drop then stop at Barock.
✉ Pařižská 24
☎ 222 329 221

Chez Marcel K-KK
This country café-restaurant serves up typical bistro fare. It is specially popular among Czech expats.
✉ Hastalska 12
☎ 222 315 676

Country Life K
Healthy eating and food shopping in the heart of the Old Town.
✉ Melantrichova 15
☎ 224 213 366

Flambée KKK
One of the most exclusive restaurants in the city that boasts Mick Jagger, Michael Jackson and Tom Cruise as its guests. The food is divine in taste, imagination and presentation. The dining room is a blend of stone-vaulted walls and plush velvet, together with a live pianist in the evening. Book in advance and dress smartly for an evening to remember. Non-smoking.
✉ Husova 5
☎ 224 248 512
ⓦ www.flambee.cz

Klub Architektů KK
A tranquil setting away from the bustle of the Old Town, with a summer terrace, a cosy cellar setting in winter, and traditional Prague cuisine all year round.
✉ Betlémské náměstí 5A
☎ 224 401 214

Kolkovna KK

A crowded and popular pub-cum-restaurant, serving hearty Czech favourites such as goulash, washed down with local Pilsner beer.

- ✉ V Kolkovně 8
- ☎ 224 819 701
- ⓦ www.kolkovna.cz

Konvikt K

A consistently popular pub/café usually full of people reading newspapers or gossiping over a cup of tea or coffee. A fine place to soak up the Prague lifestyle.

- ✉ Bartolomejská 11
- ☎ 266 711 537

Lotos KK

One of the rare restaurants for vegetarians in this meat-obsessed nation, serving up to its promise of innovative dishes.

- ✉ Platnéřská 13
- ☎ 222 322 390

Obecní dům K

As befitting its setting within the beautiful Municipal House, this 1930s-style café is incredibly grand, decorated with pillars, chandeliers and fountains. Enjoy the background piano music as you make your selection from the mouthwatering array of cakes and pastries.

- ✉ Náměstí republiky 5
- ☎ 222 002 763

Parnas KKK

The highlight of this Old Town restaurant is the striking views of the castle and Charles Bridge. The food is excellent too.

- ✉ Smetanovo nábřeží 2
- ☎ 224 239 604

Plzeňská Restaurace KK

This traditional Czech restaurant is in the basement of the Municipal House. Most people come here for the atmosphere in an elegant art nouveau setting, as well as the food.

- ✉ Náměstí republiky 5
- ☎ 222 002 770
- ⓦ www.francouzskarestaurace.cz

Potrefená Husa K

This is one of several branches of the "Shot Goose" – bright, cheerful and very contemporary bars, with an exciting menu to satisfy both locals and visitors.

- ✉ Bílkova 5
- ☎ 222 326 626

Red Hot & Blues K-KK

Cajun chicken, creole gumbo and other southern American specialities find a place on the table here. There's also live jazz and blues in the evenings. A charming and intimate place.

- ✉ Jakubská 12
- ☎ 222 314 639

Rybi trh KKK

A sumptuous fish restaurant where you'll find all the special Prague favourites in the enchanting Týn Court.

- ✉ Týn 5
- ☎ 224 895 447

Slavia K

A recent renovation has sadly stripped much of Slavia's original atmosphere where Václav Havel and fellow members of the Civic Forum once huddled to discuss their plans for defeating the Communists. It remains popular, however, largely for its wonderful views.

- ✉ Smetanovo nábřeží 2
- ☎ 224 218 493
- ⓦ www.cafeslavia.cz

Století K

When was the last time stuffed avocado reminded you of Greta Garbo? Or baked turkey breast of Harry Truman? At this quirky place, the dishes are named after the famous, with a Czech twist.

- ✉ Karoliny Světlé 12
- ☎ 222 220 008

U Medvídků K

A long-standing tourist favourite, which means that the service is a little brash and the traditional Czech food, such as pork and dumplings, is mass produced and bland. But it's worth a visit to see one of the oldest beer halls in the city, dating from the 16th century. There's also a small pension hotel upstairs.

✉ Na Perštýně 7
☎ 224 211 916
ᴡ www.umedvidku.cz

U Vejvodů K

This old pub has been remodelled, enlarged and cleaned up, and now the Pilsner hangout appeals to locals and vistors alike.

✉ Jelská 4
☎ 224 219 999
ᴡ www.restauraceuvejvoducz

HRADČANY

Bellavista KK

Reopened as a part of the reputable Kolkovna group, the Bellavista more than lives up to its name. Perched on the edge of the Strahov Monastery, it has a summer terrace with a glorious panorama of Prague. The cuisine is international but with an Italian touch.

✉ Strahovské nadvoří 1
☎ 220 517 274
ᴡ www.bella-vista.cz

Lobkowicz Palace Café K

This aristocratic establishment occupies a couple of tastefully decorated rooms in a private palace forming part of the castle complex. Visit the balcony for garden views.

✉ Jiřská 3, Pražskýhrad
☎ 602 595 998

U Zlaté hrušky KKK

One of the most elegant dining options in the city in an otherwise overly touristy area, and a favourite of international stars and politicians. Try the roast duck with pears or the beef fillet with cranberries, or for dessert the cream cheese dumplings with plum sauce. There's an extensive wine list too. Booking ahead is essential.

✉ Nový svět 3
☎ 220 514 778
ᴡ www.uzlatehrusky.cz

JOSEFOV

Franz Kafka Café K

Named after the famous writer, a native of Prague, this is a very traditional and cosy café that pays homage to the area, and offers traditional Czech cuisine.

✉ Široká 12
☎ 222 318 945

La Veranda KK

The best fusion between Czech and French cuisine in the city. A little bit pretentious, but there's good use of fresh ingredients and some innovative ideas.

✉ Elišky krásnohorské 2
☎ 224 814 733
ᴡ www.laveranda.cz

MALÁ STRANA

Café Savoy KK

Another former haunt of Franz Kafka's (if the tourist board is to be believed the man must never have stood still), this is an elegant traditional café with chandeliers and fountain.

✉ Vitézná 5
☎ 257 311 562
ᴡ www.ambi.cz

David KKK

Excellent Czech fare in an incredibly upper-class setting. Popular with politicians and local celebrities. Wild boar and rabbit are among the specialities. Remember to book ahead and dress smartly.

✉ Tržiště 21
☎ 257 533 109
ᴡ www.restaurant-david.cz

Kampa Park KKK

On a fine day there can be few nicer places to dine than the outside terrace with its views of Charles Bridge. The menu is truly international, from Czech to Oriental, but with a focus on fish and seafood.

✉ Na Kampě 8B
☎ 257 532 685

Malostranská beseda K

A traditional pub-cum-restaurant, serving Czech favourites in a vaulted hall.

✉ Malostranské náměstí 21
☎ 257 533 968
🅦 www.malostranskabeseda.cz

Pálffy palác KK

Set in a converted baroque aristocratic house with its own terrace, the restaurant offers an international and varied menu with influences from Europe, Africa and the Far East. A good choice for a special occasion.

✉ Valdštejnská 14
☎ 257 530 522
🅦 www.palffy.cz

U Kocoura K

A long-standing and perennially popular beer house between the Lower Quarter and the castle.

✉ Nerudova 2
☎ 257 530 107

U Malířů KKK

A stunning setting, resembling a medieval banqueting hall, and a mouthwatering menu with a French influence. The tasting menus offer smaller dishes with more courses so you can sample the full expertise of the chef. Booking is essential.

✉ Maltézské náměstí 11
☎ 257 530 000
🅦 www.umaliru.cz

U Sedmi švábů KK

This medieval pub enthusiastically serves up Czech specialities such as pork knuckle, accompanied by Bohemian folk music.

✉ Jánský vršek 14
☎ 257 531 455

NOVÉ MĚSTO

Alcron KKK

One of the best places in Prague for fish and seafood, including that great Czech favourite, pike-perch. An intimate restaurant within the Radisson SAS hotel.

✉ Štěpánská 40
☎ 222 820 000

Café Louvre K

A traditional Prague coffee house, once frequented by Franz Kafka and other literati, serving all day from breakfast to dinner. The menu is simple, traditional Czech fare.

✉ Národní 20
☎ 224 930 949
🅦 www.cafelouvre.cz

Celnice K

In the splendid old Customs House, this is one of Pilsner Urquell's expertly remodelled pubs. People love the Bohemian cuisine.

✉ V Celenici 4
☎ 224 212 240

Cicala KK

The unrivalled reputation of Cicala as the best Italian restaurant in the city is in no small part due to the ingredients being shipped in direct from Italy – everything from the olive oil to the parmesan to the sun-baked tomatoes and figs.

✉ Žitná 43
☎ 222 210 375
🅦 www.trattoria.cicala.cz

Dobromila KK

Czech ingredients are given a distinctive French twist in this fusion restaurant.

✉ Jungmannova 10
☎ 296 246 464

Govinda Vegetarian Club K

Plenty of whole food at this Hare Krishna

restaurant-cum-bakery-cum-tea room. Its attraction lies in its location, not far off from the art noveau Municipal House.

✉ Soukenicka 27
☎ 224 816 016

Hybernia K

The latest, and in this case, particularly successful attempt to present decent Czech cuisine to discerning local and international diners. You can dine on the ground floor, in the courtyard or cellar.

✉ Hybrenská 7
☎ 224 226 004
Ⓦ www.hybernia.cz

Kavárna Evropa KK

The art nouveau interior attached to the famous Evropa Hotel is also one of the sights of Prague. Though service has not always matched the surroundings and the restaurant does sometimes ask for a cover charge, the place is simply stunning.

✉ Václavske náměstí 25
☎ 224 215 387
Ⓦ www.evropahotel.cz

Na rybárně KK

Similar to Alcron, this is a top choice in Prague if you want fish and seafood.

✉ Gorazdova 17
☎ 224 918 885

Novoměstský pivovar K

A cavernous pub with its own brewery, serving simple but filling food. It tends to be noisy, but is good for groups.

✉ Vodičkova 20
☎ 222 232 448
Ⓦ www.npivovar.cz

La Perle du Prague KKK

Located atop the controversial "Fred and Ginger" building, this sophisticated restaurant serves mostly French cuisine. Great views of the city and river.

✉ Rašinovo nábřeži 80
☎ 221 984 160

Pod Křídlem KKK

A classy restaurant close to the National Theatre, it offers stylish surroundings, a great atmosphere and the choicest international cuisine.

✉ Národní 10 (entrance from Voršilská)
☎ 224 933 571

U Fleků K

Czech stalwarts such as roast pork, sauerkraut and dumplings or beef in cream sauce are the mainstay of the menu in what is one of the oldest breweries in the city. A great favourite with tourists and often crowded with tour groups.

✉ Křemencová 11
☎ 224 934 019
Ⓦ www.ufleku.cz

U Kalicha K

This pub achieved international fame when it was mentioned in Jaroslav Hašek's novel *The Good Soldier Švejk*, one of the most popular books ever written by a Czech author. Today the pub is adorned with articles and images relating to the book and, as such, draws crowds of tourists.

✉ Na Bojiští 12
☎ 296 189 600

U Šuterů KKK

A cosy place specialising in Czech cuisine with treats like roast duck, roast pork and fruit dumplings.

✉ Palackého 4
☎ 224 947 120

FURTHER AFIELD

Hanavský Pavilon KKK

This garden restaurant in the neo-baroque pavilion in the heart of Letná Park offers a truly Czech experience, with classic Czech dining, enhanced by piano music and wonderful views of the city centre.

✉ Letenské sady 173
☎ 233 323 641
Ⓦ www.hanavskypavilon.cz

Shopping

Shopping in Prague is one of the many pleasures of a visit to the city. The most obvious, if not the easiest, souvenir to take home is a piece of the world-famous Bohemian glass, but many of the gift shops in the city centre also sell a variety of other items, with an emphasis on wood and textiles.

Bohemian garnets are also well known and various jewellers are dotted around the city, particularly in the New Town. The New Town, in and around Wenceslas Square, is the main commercial area of Prague, where you'll find most of the department stores, as well as international brands such as Benetton, Zara and H&M. The Malá Strana area is the place to head for if you're looking for exclusive one-off boutiques and small art galleries.

In summer there are also a lot of open-air stalls, particularly in the Old Town and on and around Charles Bridge, many of which sell hand-crafted gifts such as ceramic Prague houses, and in some cases, memorabilia from the Communist regime. There is a daily fruit and vegetable market in the Old Town, while outside the centre is where you'll find the large-scale shopping centres and the largest market, in Holešovice.

Credit cards are increasingly accepted, but in some of the smaller shops and certainly at stalls, you will have to pay cash.

Opening hours, unless otherwise listed, are usually Monday to Friday 9am to 6pm, and Saturday 9am to 1pm, though in very popular areas, the hours may be longer and shops remain open on Sunday too.

STARÉ MĚSTO

Alma Antique
Rambling old-fashioned, ground-floor and basement establishment with every conceivable kind of antique object. Great place to pick up a souvenir.
✉ Valentinská 7
☎ 224 813 991

Antikvariát Pařižská
One of the few shops on this prestigious boulevard not dealing in designer labels,

with walls papered with antique maps, old prints and posters.

✉ **Pařižská 8**
☎ 222 321 442

Art Deco

Glass, ceramics, jewellery, clothing and more from the 1920s and 1930s. Prices are high but don't be afraid to negotiate with the owner.

✉ **Michalská 21**
☎ 224 223 076

Big Ben Bookshop

One of Prague's institutions, this is where you'll find a great selection of guidebooks and Czech literature. A charming bookshop, full of character.

✉ **Malá Štupartská 5**
☎ 224 826 565

Botanicus

Organic products – soaps, cosmetics, teas, herbs and spices – produced on a farm in Lysá nad Labem under the expert supervision of a British specialist. Botanicus has several other outlets, including one in the Týn Courtyard.

✉ **Michalská 2**
☎ 224 212 977

Celetná Crystal

Bohemian and cut glass are world-renowned and this is one of the most popular places to buy them. Just make sure that the shop assistants pack it well enough to travel.

✉ **Celetná 15**
☎ 224 811 376

Clockhouse

A popular fashion stop, decked out in a similar way to popular high street stores H&M and Mango, complete with innovative design touches, and generally catering to teenage girls.

✉ **Na Příkopé 3**
☎ 224 242 527

Dorotheum

If you're interested in antiques try to attend an auction at this renowned auction house. The collections vary: jewellery, art, clocks and more. Even if you don't buy anything, just come for the experience.

✉ **Ovocný trh 2**
☎ 224 222 001

Dům Vín Ceské Rupubliky

Wine gourmands shouldn't miss this one. It's the "Winehouse of the Czech Republic" and offers for a fee tastings from its huge range of Bohemian and Moravian vintages.

✉ **Týn 7**
☎ 224 827 155

Granát Turnov

Even though Prague may not be your idea of a jewellery mecca, this is one of the city's best jewellery stores, specialising in Bohemian garnets cast into traditional settings. You'll be pleasantly surprised and perhaps even tempted to buy something small – or big!

✉ **Dlouhá 28–30**
☎ 222 315 612

Havelské trziste

For just the smells, sounds and colours of a local market, visit this one, open daily in the Old Town, for fresh fruit and vegetables.

✉ **Havelská 13**
☎ 224 239 331

Ivana Follová Art & Fashion

A large shop in the Týn Courtyard offering high-end, locally made silk dresses and scarves. The shop also has some beautifully crafted ceramics.

✉ **Týn 1 (between Týnská and Stupartská)**
☎ 224 895 460

Manufaktura

There are a number of branches of this gift shop around the city, which specialises in hand-crafted gifts and souvenirs, with an emphasis on wood, textiles and ceramics.

Here you can pick up traditional and unusual items both from the region and further afield.

✉ Melantrichova 17
☎ 221 632 480

Moser

A visit to this famed shop is a must. Glassware long produced in the Czech district of Karlovy Vary is on sale here.

✉ Na Prikope 12
☎ 224 222 012

Tupesy

Charming folk ceramics from Moravia, sold to the sound of *cembalorn*, the folk-music of the region. The shop lends a quaint touch to Haveská Street.

✉ Haveská 21
☎ 224 214 176

Wilvorst

A designer fashion shop, selling its own label. as well as those of other well-known names, such as Jean Paul Gautier.

✉ U Prasné brány 3
☎ 222 323 573

HRADČANY

CDMusic.cz

A small and welcoming record establishment in the arcade on the south side of Loretta Square, specialising in "Czech labels at Czech prices". It stocks an impressive collection of Western classical music, as well some of the wonderful jazz that has come out of Prague.

✉ Siroký dvůr, Loretánské náměstí 4
☎ 220 515 403

Gambra

Specially for discerning book-and-art lovers; this little Nový svět gallery has intriguing art objects and books.

✉ Černínská 5
☎ 220 514 527

Zlatá Ulička

Even though you have to pay to get in (tickets are available from the Castle ticket counter), the picturesque Golden Lane, lined with quaint shops and cheerful cottages, is worth visiting if you are in search of usual and unusual souvenirs. The tiny buildings have been turned into shops selling a variety of items, among them (at shop No 23) a fascinating collection of antique prints, posters and maps.

✉ Zlatá Ulička, Pražský hrad

JOSEFOV

Navarila

Prague isn't much of a fashion capital in terms of clothes, but this is one of the nicest boutiques, which sells collections by the Czech designer Martina Nevařilová.

✉ Elisky Krásnohorské 4
☎ 271 742 091

MALÁ STRANA

Blue Praha

A lovely gift shop selling blown glass in all guises: tableware, vases, bathroom accessories. Conveniently, they can also arrange shipping.

✉ Mostecká 24
☎ 257 533 716

Obchod s Loutkami

A handicraft lover's paradise, this is where you'll get some of the finest handmade puppets in Prague. Some of the individual designs can be expensive, but many others are reasonably priced. The shop is supplied by over 30 craftspeople.

✉ Nerudova 47
☎ 257 532 735

Josef Katrák

If you're passionate about old things, especially from this part of Europe, this shop is a real find. It has an eclectic mix of antiques, selling everything from furniture and jewellery to 1920s' posters and old photographs.

✉ Nerudova 51
☎ 257 532 200

Pavla a Olga

One of the original and innovative design retail outlets of the acclaimed fashion designer and stylists Pavla and Olga. Exclusive and very East European – also expensive.

✉ Vlašská 13
☎ 728 939 872

NOVÉ MĚSTO

Academia

A really interesting variety of photography books, travel guides, cookbooks and literature in English can be found at this specialist bookshop.

✉ Václavské náměstí 34
☎ 224 223 511

Antikvariát Galerie Mustek

This old established firm in the shopping arcade of the Adria Palace is a typical example of the Prague Antikvariát (antiquarian bookshop), with not just books but a fascinating selection of maps and prints as well.

✉ Národní třída 40
☎ 224 949 587

Bílá labuť

Prague's most established department store, selling everything you would expect, from fashion to household goods. There's also a branch on Wenceslas Square.

✉ Na Poříčí 23
☎ 222 327 905

Bontonland Koruna

This is reputedly the biggest music shop in Central Europe. It is situated in the labyrinthine basement of the Koruna Palace at the corner of Wenceslas Square and Na přikopě.

✉ Václavské náměstí 1
☎ 224 473 080

Botanicus

A very popular shop for all things organic, from soaps and cosmetics to herbs, incense and tea.

✉ Týnský dvůr 3, Ungelt
☎ 224 895 446

Cellarius

In the Lucerna arcade off Wenceslas Square, this well-stocked shop sells wines from around the world, as well as from the vineyards of Bohemia and Moravia.

✉ Štepánská 61
☎ 224 210 979

Galerie Pyramida

Not all Czech glass is for serving wine. This spacious shop displays art glass from some of the best Czech designers. There are also other *objets d'art*, including beautiful small bronzes for sale.

✉ Národní 11
☎ 224 213 117

Globe Bookstore and Café

Reputedly one of the best places in the city for English-language books, which you are encouraged to peruse at leisure in this shop-cum-café.

✉ Pstrossova 6
☎ 224 934 203

Halada

Much of the jewellery on sale in Prague is of traditional design, but Halada sells more modern pieces. Their silverware is particularly attractive.

✉ Na Příkopě 16
☎ 224 221 304

Kiwi

A travel agency and a map store, Kiwi offers a comprehensive range of maps and guides to the Czech Republic and beyond. Check out their basement where you'll find

a fascinating collection of wall maps.
✉ Jungmannova 23
☎ 224 948 455

Kotva

Looking for an everyday or perhaps an
unusual utility item? Maybe a penknife or a
nice wine set? Then this is another
long-established department store
that also includes a supermarket.
✉ Náměstí republiky 8
☎ 224 801 111

Modrobílá linie

A quirky gift shop selling an eclectic
range of items, from food to ceramics
to household bric-à-brac, all beautifully
packaged for giving.
✉ Stepánská 61
☎ 224 213 710

Myslivost

This shop caters to wildlife and outdoor
lovers. If you're looking for durable outdoor
furniture, rucksacks, sleeping bags,
camping equipment, clothes and shoes,
there are many things you may like to buy
at this well-stocked outlet.
✉ Jungmannova 25
☎ 224 949 014

Palác Knih Luxor

There is no reason to dispute the claim of
the "Palace of Books" to be the biggest
in the country. When you descend to the
basement you'll find titles in English and
other languages. The firm has another store
in the Nový Smichov mall.
✉ Václavské náměří 41
☎ 221 111 364

Tesco

Rival to Kotva and once bearing the
impeccably proletarian name of "Maj" (May),
this department store is now in British
hands. A ride up the escalator gives an
excellent view of downtown. The basement
supermarket is the busiest in town.

✉ Národní 26
☎ 222 003 111

FURTHER AFIELD

Obchodní Centrum Nový Smíchov

If you're staying away from the centre of
town, you'll find this a useful place to visit.
It's a large shopping centre and includes
fashion stores with some international
names, as well as restaurants, cafés,
bookstores and a hypermarket.
✉ Plzenská 8, Smíchov
☎ 251 511 151

Prazská trznice Holešovice

Another fascinating place to look around
and absorb atmosphere of Prague. It's
the largest market place in the area, just
outside the city centre north of the river.
Take note: it's closed on Sundays.
✉ Bubenské nábřeží 306, Holešovice
☎ 220 800 945

Entertainment

Praguers take entertainment and culture very seriously, but that is not to say that they are snobbish about what is high-brow and low-brow. Cultural entertainment – classical music, opera, ballet and theatre – has a year-round programme in the city, featuring the very best of both Czech and international performers.

The National Theatre is a beloved institution and the two greatest concert venues, the Smetana Hall in the Municipal House and the Dvořák Hall in the Rudolfinum, are named in honour of two of the nation's greatest composers. Folk music is also popular. Look out for Folklórní Skupina in the city listings. Then there is the experimental theatre, in particular the Black Light genre that involves mime and special effects, while puppetry is an on-going art.

Praguers love to party, especially in summer, when nightclubs, discos and jazz clubs keep up the beat until daybreak.

The city has a year-round calendar of cultural events, the most famous of these being the Prague Spring Festival, which traditionally begins on 12 May with a performance of Smetana's *Má Vlast* (*My Country*), and closes on 3 June with Beethoven's *Ninth Symphony*. The Prague

Autumn Festival and other chamber, opera, and varied events keep up the rhythm in a rich programme of music.

Other major events include the Days of European Film from late January to early February, the Febiofest of Czech film in the same month, an International Book Fair in February, a summer Shakespeare Festival and an International Jazz Festival each October. It's rare that you will find yourself in Prague without at least one festival going on, even if on a smaller scale.

The best way to find out what's happening during your stay is either to visit the tourist office, get hold of the English-language newspaper *The Prague Post* or log on to www.praguepost.com. Apart from various ticket agents, there's a ticket office called Ticketpro within the Old Town Hall. Telephone for opening timings or consult www.ticketpro.cz.

STARÉ MĚSTO

Agharta Jazz Centrum
Czech jazz musicians as well as international groups from as far as Cuba and Brazil frequent this popular music club. It also plays host to the annual jazz festival in the city each spring.
✉ Železná 16
☎ 222 211 275

All Colours Theatre
Black Light theatre, which combines film projections with live actors and special-effects lighting has been popular in Prague for more than 50 years and this is one of the main venues to see it.
✉ Rytířská 31
☎ 221 610 114

Batalion Music Pub
A loud and thumping disco-cum-live venue, as well as an internet café and sports bar.
✉ 28 Října 3
☎ 220 108 147

Betlémská kaple
Like so many religious buildings around the city, the Bethlehem Chapel stages regular classical music concerts in summer. Mozart and Dvořák are hot favourites on the calendar of events, which is available from the tourist office.
✉ Betlémské náměstí 4
☎ 224 248 595

Divadlo Ta Fantastika Praha
Another popular Black Light theatre venue that also stages musicals.
✉ Karlova 8
☎ 222 221 366

Double Trouble
You can dance until the early hours in this rowdy cellar bar with live DJs. Definitely only for the young.
✉ Melantrichova 17
☎ 221 632 414

Klementium
This vast complex hosts chamber concerts in its halls of mirrors (Zracidlowá siň).
✉ Entances at Karlova 1, Mariánské náměstí and Křižovnické náměsti
☎ 221 663 111

Klub Lávka
A combined restaurant, theatre and nightclub. The dance floor of the latter spills out on to a terrace that has wonderful views of the Charles Bridge.
✉ Novotného lávaka 1
☎ 221 082 299

Kostel sv Mikuláše
The Old Town's St Nicholas Church is a lovely setting for classical music concerts in spring and summer. Programmes are available from the tourist office, but there are usually posters and people handing out flyers near the church to tell you what's on and the best times to go.
✉ Staroměstské náměstí
☎ 224 190 991

N11
Another lively nightclub, with different music genres played by live DJs on different nights, from house music and hip-hop to 1980s nostalgia and R'n'B.
✉ Národní 11
☎ 222 075 705

Národni divadlo marionet
This is a truly Czech experience. Mozart's great opera *Don Giovanni* is performed here with marionettes dressed in period costume by the National Marionette Theatre.
✉ Žatecká 1
☎ 224 819 322

Obcení dům
The Smetana Hall of the Municipal House is one of the most beautiful and important concert venues in the city.
✉ Náměstí republiky 5
☎ 222 002 101

Roxy

Unusual underground DJs and live acts of every conceivable sort, including stars of the music world, can be heard here.

✉ Dlouhá 33
☎ 224 826 296

Rudolfinum

Home to the Czech Philharmonic Orchestra, which performs here in the lovely Dvořák Hall. This is also one of the main venues for the Prague Spring Festival.

✉ Alšova nábreží 12
☎ 227 059 111

Stavovské divadlo

The Estates Theatre saw the premiere of Mozart's *Don Giovanni*, which he wrote in Prague in 1787. Today it stages ballet and drama from around the world, but performances are in Czech.

✉ Ovocný trh 1
☎ 224 901 448

Ta Fantastika

Another spectacle based on the Black Light fusion of dance, mime and music – a spin-off from the hugely successful and famous *Laterna Magika* (Magic Lantern).

✉ Karlova 8
☎ 222 221 366

Ungelt Jazz & Blues Club

Touring jazz musicians play in this 15th-century cellar bar seven nights a week.

✉ Týnská ulička 2
☎ 224 895 748

U Staré paní

Praguers love jazz and in this jazz lounge you can enjoy musicians from all over the world, while sipping cocktails.

✉ Michalská 9
☎ 603 551 680

Vagon

All night and every night you can listen to rock or reggae in this dive on the Old Town side of Národní třída. Get ready to dance the night away at this disco.

✉ Narodni trida 25
☎ 221 085 599

HRADČANY

Bazilika sv Jiří

St George's Basilica provides a striking setting for classical music concerts, usually chamber music. Concerts are also held in St George's Convent.

✉ Náměstí U Svatého Jiří
☎ 224 373 368

MALÁ STRANA

Chrám sv Mikuláše

Mozart once played the organ at the beautiful baroque St Nicholas' Church, so it's a fitting venue for classical concerts, particularly of Mozart's works.

✉ Malostranské náměstí
☎ 257 534 215

Lichtenstejnsky palac

The beautiful Lichtenstein Palace is a perfect setting for the symphony orchestra and other recitals staged here. Home to the Prague Music Academy, it often stages student performances.

✉ Malostranské náměstí 13
☎ 257 535 568

U Malěho Glena

Little Glen is named after its genial owner who plays recorded jazz in the upstairs bar, and the real thing – alternating with pop or rock acts – in the basement. What a great atmosphere and crowd!

✉ Karmelitská 23
☎ 257 531 717

NOVÉ MĚSTO

Akkord

A new hip dance club near the Municipal House, featuring everything from funk rock to jazz grooves. A favourite with locals and visitors alike who love to dance.

✉ Celnici 4
☎ 774 101 091

Divadlo Animato

Another Black Light theatre, staging performances with a less traditional theme – such as the acclaimed foot-tapping "Story of the Beatles".

✉ Na Přikopé 10
☎ 222 244 358

Kino Lucerna

The Grand Hall of the Lucerna Palace has witnessed performances from such greats as Ella Fitzgerald, Louis Armstrong and Yehudi Menuhin, and concerts are still staged in this plush setting. There's also a restaurant and an elegant shopping arcade. Book well in advance.

✉ Štěpánská 61
☎ 224 216 972

Laterna Magika

The first and most famous of Prague's many Black Light theatres, begun in 1958 and still going strong.

✉ Národní 4
☎ 222 222 039

Metropolitan Jazz Club

Another of Prague's many jazz venues, with an emphasis on swing, blues and jazz violin. Young and upcoming groups have made their debut here.

✉ Jungmannova 14
☎ 224 947 777

Národní divadlo

The National Theatre, on the banks of the Vltava, is undoubtedly the most important entertainment venue for the Czech people because it was built in anticipation of their independence. Drama, ballet and opera are all staged here.

✉ Národní 2
☎ 224 901 111

Reduta Jazz Club

The most popular of Prague's many jazz venues, with live music seven nights a week.

✉ Národní 20
☎ 224 933 487

Rock Café

A performance venue for indie bands – expect rock, grunge, punk, and a lot of noise. Definitely for the young and energetic.

✉ Národní 116
☎ 224 933 947

Státní opera Praha

The main opera venue in the city, the state's opera house largely stages classical works such as *Aida*, *The Barber of Seville* and *Turandot*. Ballet is also performed here.

✉ Legerova 75
☎ 296 117 111

FURTHER AFIELD

Bertramka

Mozart concerts are staged in summer in the house that the composer once occupied, which is now a museum dedicated to his time in Prague.

✉ Mozartova 169, Smíchov
☎ 257 317 465

Cinema City Flora

All the main large-scale cinema complexes are located outside the city centre, and this is one of the most popular. The screenings are usually in English, with Czech subtitles. There's also an IMAX cinema screen within the complex.

✉ Vinohradská 149, Žižkov
☎ 255 742 021

Sazka Arena

Prague's main arena stadium is the setting for touring rock bands, sports events and other large-scale shows.

✉ Ocelářská 460, Vysočany
☎ 266 771 000

Travel Facts

Prague has undergone major changes since 1990, making it a much more tourist-friendly city than it has been in the past. Though language can be an obstacle in smaller establishments, English is increasingly understood, and with rapid modernisation many of the services are easier to access and operate independently. Nevertheless, it is always useful to have an idea of some of the practical aspects of being in the city, which will make your visit much more enjoyable.

ARRIVING

By Air

A number of scheduled airlines operate services in and out of Prague, including British Airways (www.britishairways.com), Air France (www.airfrance.com) and Czech Airlines (www.csa.cz). The no-frills airline easyJet (www.easyjet.com) also runs a service to Prague at very low prices.

The airport is 20km (12.5 miles) west of the city centre. Counters offer information and money exchange services; there are ATMs, car and taxi hire facilities, a left-luggage help desk and other essential services. There is also a post office in the Administrative Centre across the car park.

By Bus and Taxi

Shuttle buses run at regular 15-minute intervals between the Praha Ruzyná airport and Náměstí Republiky in the Old Town. Remember that backpacks or suitcases will require a half ticket. Minibuses also operate from outside the arrivals area and tickets can be bought directly from the driver. Minibuses can also be booked by telephone for the airport.

Taxis are also available outside the arrivals area, with the fares payable to the airport authorities – these can be paid by VISA credit card, and the drivers usually understand some English.

By Train

Trains from most of the major European capitals arrive and depart at the main station Hlavní nádraží (or Wilsonova). For travellers on a budget there are also coach services between Prague and major European destinations that arrive and depart at the Florenc bus station in the New Town.

CALENDAR OF EVENTS

On the following public holidays, banks, post offices, business offices, department stores and shops remain closed:

1 January New Year's Day
Mar/April Easter Monday
1 May Labour Day
8 May Liberation Day
5 July Cyril and Methodius Day
6 July Jan Hus Day
28 September St Wenceslas' Day
28 October Day of the Republic
17 November Day of the Struggle for Liberty and Democracy
24 December Christmas Eve
25 December Christmas Day
26 December St Stephen's Day

CLIMATE

Prague has a mild spring and summer and a crisp and cold winter, usually with snow. The average temperature in January is -1°C (28°F); the average temperature in July is 18°C (65°F). Warm clothes, including hats, scarves and gloves, are essential in winter, but even in summer it is advisable to bring a warm jacket as the temperature is changeable. Walking shoes are needed to cope with the miles of cobbled streets.

CUSTOMS

Members of the EU have an unlimited allowance as long as they can prove goods are for personal use or gifts and are not for re-sale. For visitors from other countries the allowance is 200 cigarettes or 100 cigars or 250g of tobacco per person, 2 litres of wine, 1 litre of spirits and any other items up to a value of Kč6,000. Purchases made in Prague will carry a customs duty on departure if they are valued at more than Kč30,000. Be careful about taking out genuine antiques – they should be certified by the National Museum or the Museum of Decorative Arts. You may bring in as much currency as you wish but cash exceeding Kč350,000 must be declared.

DISCOUNTS

The Prague Card, available from tourist offices, is a useful item to buy if you plan to visit a great number of museums and monuments. Valid for a four-day period it covers the admission cost to more than 50 sights, including the most popular.

DRIVING

No visitor should consider driving in Prague's central zones. Travel to the city centre is best by public transport. Especially avoid driving out of (Fridays) and into (Sundays) the city at weekends. Much of the area is pedestrianised, the streets are narrow and crowded and the one-way systems and lack of parking spaces are infuriating. If you are bringing your own car into the city, it is best to leave it in one of the suburbs, in a secure car park (car theft is a serious issue and though there are paid, convenient car parks, few of them are actually guarded). Car robbers look out especially for cars bearing foreign number plates, so be sure to bring a reliable locking device for your car.

The Prague Information Service publishes a useful guide for drivers called

Transport Guide. Remember that trams have the right of way and you can only overtake one from the right and only if the tram is in motion.

There are several car rental companies. You must be over 21, in possession of a valid international car licence and have been driving for at least one year before you will be allowed to rent a car. You must have both ID and a credit card.

ELECTRICITY

Electricity in Prague is 230 volts and sockets are served by European two-pin plugs. Adaptors are available in electrical stores and at airport shops.

EMBASSIES

Australia: Klimentska 10, Nové Město
Tel: 296 578 350
Canada: Muchova 6, Bubenec
Tel: 272 101 800
France: Velkopěrovské náměstí 2,
Malá Strana
Tel: 251 171 711
Great Britain: Thunovská 14
Malá Strana
Tel: 257 402 111
Ireland: Tržiště 13, Malá Strana
Tel: 257 530 061
Russia: Náměstí Pod Kaštany 1, Bubenec
Tel: 233 374 100
South Africa: Ruská 65, Vrsovice
Tel: 267 311 114
USA: Tržiště 15, Mala Strana
Tel: 257 022 000

EMERGENCY TELEPHONE NUMBERS

Ambulance: 155
Car breakdown: 1230/1240
Doctor (emergency service): 155
EU-wide emergency hotline: 112
Fire: 150
Emergency dental service: 224 946 981
Municipal police: 156
Police: 158

GETTING AROUND

Metro

The most convenient way of getting around Prague, other than on foot, is the fast and efficient metro system. It operates between 5am and midnight. There are three lines – A (green), B (yellow) and C (red) – that serve the city centre and the immediate suburbs such as Žižkov and Vyšehrad. The metro stations used most by tourists exploring the city are Můstek, Staroměstská and Malonstranská. Stations are marked by a green M sign set within a triangle.

Maps and detailed guides in English are on sale. Tickets can be bought from counters at the station and from newsstands, snack shops, hotels and information offices. Children under six can travel free, though you must pay extra for a large suitcase or backpack. Tickets should to be stamped by a machine at the metro station in order to validate them for travel within specified time limits (60 minutes between 5am and 8pm on weekdays and 90 minutes any other time). There is unlimited transfers between all kinds of transport. Be sure to have valid tickets, as you could be checked at any time by inspectors in plain clothes.

Tram, bus and taxi

Prague also operates tram and bus routes. Some lines operate all night. The most commonly used tram routes are 14, 17 and 22, which cover all the main sights. Buses do not run in the city centre because of the narrowness of many streets, but are a convenient way to visit the suburbs. Taxis are available but tend to be an expensive option in a city that is so easily navigable by other means.

GUIDED TOURS

Pragotur, in the Old Town Hall in the Old Town Square, offers English-language guides who will take you around the city, either on a general tour or with specific themes, such as churches or architecture (tel: 236 002 562; www.prague-info.cz).

Alternatively, you can join one of the Prague Sightseeing Tours' buses that leave from Náměstí republicky at various times of the day. This is an excellent idea if you're short of time and want to get the most out of the city from an experienced guide (tel: 222 314 655; www.pstours.cz).

Organised trips to popular sights outside the city, such as Karlštejn Castle or Karlovy Vary, can be arranged at the tourist office.

HEALTH FACILITIES

All visitors, including non-EU members, are entitled to free emergency treatment; for any other treatment it is important to have medical insurance. Medical services for EU citizens are cheaper than for others or even free if there is a reciprocal agreement (check when leaving your country). If you are on regular medication in your home country, make sure you bring enough supplies to last your trip and a prescription that gives details of the generic name of the medicine, as well as the trade name.

The main hospital serving Prague is the Hospital Na Homolce at Roentgenova 2, on the road to Pilsen (tel: 257 272 146). There is also a health centre in the New Town, Poliklinika Na Národní (Národní 9, tel: 222 075 120). A 24-hour pharmacy (*lékarná*) can be found in the New Town at Palackého 5 (tel: 224 946 982) and the American Dental Associates are in the Nové Město area (metro: Náměstí Republiky, tel: 221 181 121).

LANGUAGE

Czech is a member of the Slavic group of languages, such as Slovakian, Polish and Russian. No one expects visitors to speak Czech, but, using a few words and phrases will be greatly appreciated and will help in reading signs. The stress is always on the first syllable of a word. However, English is steadily becoming more common, especially among younger people.

Some useful words and phrases are given below, in English first and then in Czech:

Hello	Ahoj
Good morning	Dobré ráno
Good afternoon	Dobré odpoledne
Goodnight	Dobrou noc
Goodbye	Na shledanou
Please	Prosím
Thank you	Děkuji
Yes	Ano
No	Ne
Entrance	Vchod
Exit	Východ
Open	Otevřeno
Closed	Zavřeno
No smoking	Kouření Zakázáno
Do you speak English?	Mluvíte anglicky?
I don't understand	Nerozumím
Who?	Kdo?
What?	Co?
When?	Kdy?
Where?	Kde?
How?	Jak?
How much?	Kolik?
Bar	Do baru
Café	Do kavárny
Cinema	Do kina
Disco	Na diskotéku
Opera	Na operu
Restaurant	Do restaurace
Theatre	Do divadla

LAVATORIES
In pubs, restaurants, museums and galleries, the signs for lavatories may be written in Czech – *mužl* or *páni* for men; *ženy* or *dámy* for women.

LOST PROPERTY
The main lost property office for the city is in the Old Town at Karoliny Světlé 5 (tel: 224 235 085). If unretrievable, your embassy should help with a letter written in Czech, preferably for the police, which will be useful for claiming insurance. The British Embassy will arrange emergency passports for your return journey. You can also apply for a temporary replacement visa from the Foreigners' Police and Passport Office, which is in Žižkov.

MONEY MATTERS
The Czech currency is the crown (koruna or Kč), which is made up of 100 hellers. Coins come in denominations of 50 hellers and Kč1, 2, 5, 10, 20 and 50. Bank notes come in denominations of Kč20, 50, 100, 200, 500, 1000, 2000 and 5000.

You should keep coins and small denomination notes handy for use with public facilities such as telephones, in toilets and for tipping. Often smaller shops, cafés and restaurants do not have enough smaller currency to give as change for the large notes used by visitors.

Instead of carrying cash, you can use your debit cards to withdraw money at a relatively minimal charge, sometimes for free. Try and change larger amounts of money at a time to save on the commission you pay (which can be up to 2 per cent). Hotels charge more – between 5 to 8 per cent – while private exchange offices can charge up to 10 per cent. There is also a commission of about 2 per cent for changing traveller's cheques.

Larger hotels accept credit cards, which can also be used to get a cash advance from a bank.

For lost credit cards and traveller's cheques call:
Amex: 222 800 222
Diners Club: 267 197 450
MasterCard/Eurocard: 261 354 650
VISA: 272 771 111

OPENING HOURS
Banks are open Monday to Friday from 8am to 5pm.

Shops are generally open Monday to Friday from 9am to 6pm and Saturday 9am to 1pm, but many shops in the city centre, particularly in very touristy areas, may stay open later and operate daily.

The majority of museums are closed on Mondays but are open Tuesday to Sunday from 9 or 10am to 5 or 6pm. Specific opening hours for individual sights are given with their entries in this guide.

POSTAL SERVICES

The main post office in the city centre can be found in the New Town at Jindřišská 14, which is open from 2am to midnight. Smaller post offices are open Monday to Friday 8am to 6pm, Saturday 8:30–11am. Stamps can also be bought at some kiosks and at hotel receptions. Post offices do not receive parcels after noon on Saturdays and on Sundays. Do not send antiques by mail and remember that US, Australian and New Zealand post offices will not accept parcels containing glass or crystal items.

The professional courier service DHL has an office just off Wenceslas Square with staff who speak English (tel: 800 103 000, free call; www.dhl.cz).

SECURITY

Prague is a safe city as a general rule, but as always, common sense should prevail. Avoid dark, isolated streets at night and carry as little cash or valuables with you as possible. Watch for pickpockets that mill around the main tourist spots such as Prague Castle, Charles Bridge and the Old Town Square; keep your money safely, keep bags zipped up and keep a firm hold on to your camera.

TELEPHONE NUMBERS/CODES

Public telephones accept either coins (minimum Kč10) or cards that are sold at newsagents, tourist offices and post offices.

If you have a roaming facility on your mobile phone you will be able to use it in Prague via either T-Mobile, Vodafone or Telefonica networks.

For international directory enquiries dial 1181; for local directory enquiries dial 1180.

To call the UK from Prague dial 00 44 then the UK number minus the first zero; to call the Czech Republic from the UK dial 00 420, then the local number.

TIPPING

As a general rule in bars, pubs and beer houses, round the bill up to the nearest (highest) Kč10. In the more upmarket restaurants add a tip of around 10 per cent to the bill. In taxis, round up the fare.

TOURIST OFFICES

Tourist offices (listed below) are part of the Prague Information Service (tel: 12 444 or 221 714 444; www.prague-info.cz):
Staroměstské náměstí (Old Town Hall): Apr–Oct, Mon–Fri 9–7, Sat and Sun 9–6; Nov–Mar, Mon–Fri 9–6, Sat and Sun 9–5
Wilsonova 8 (Main Railway Station): Apr–Oct, Mon–Fri 9–7, Sat and Sun 9–6; Nov–Mar, Mon–Fri 9–6, Sat 9–5
Rytířská 31, Staré Mesto: Apr–Oct, daily 9–7; Nov–Mar, 9–6
Malostranské mostecké veze (Malá Strana Bridge Tower, Charles Bridge): Apr–Oct, daily 10–6

TRAVELLERS WITH DISABILITIES

A few museums provide special facilities. Traffic signals in central Prague have sound signals to indicate when it is safe to cross, and some hotels also provide the required facilities for disabled travellers. However, few buses and no trams have wheelchair access. However, there are specially equipped buses that operate during the week on line Nos 1 and 3.

Index

SPOTLIGHT ON PRAGUE

Acknowledgements

The Automobile Association would like to thank the following photographers, companies and picture libraries for their assistance in the preparation of this book.

Abbreviations for the picture credits are as follows: (t) top; (b) bottom; (l) left; (r) right; (AA) AA World Travel Library

Front Cover (across from top left, a-k)
a) River Vltava, AA/J Wyand; b) Prazsky hrad, AA/J Smith; c) Charles Bridge, AA/J Smith; d) Building detail, Vaclavske Namesti, AA/J Smith; e) Stare Mesto, AA/J Smith; f b/g) Tyn Church, AA/S McBride; g) Tancici dum, AA/J Smith; h) View from Letna, AA/J Smith; i) Staromestske namesti, AA/J Smith; j) Café Imperial, AA/J Smith; k) Narodni divadlo, AA/J Smith

3 AA/S McBride; 4l AA/J Smith; 4c AA; 4r AA/J Smith; 5l AA/J Smith; 5c AA/S McBride; 5r AA/J Smith; 6/7 AA/J Smith; 8/9 AA/S McBride; 11 AA/C Sawyer; 12t AA/J Smith; 12bl AA/S McBride; 12cr AA/S McBride; 12br AA/S McBride; 13t AA/J Smith; 13b AA/S McBride; 14t AA/J Smith; 14b AA/S McBride; 15 AA/J Smith; 16cl AA/C Sawyer; 16bl AA/S McBride; 16br AA/S McBride; 17bl AA/S McBride; 17br AA/S McBride; 18 AA/T Souter; 19 AA/J Smith; 20 AA/S McBride; 20/21 AA/S McBride; 22 AA/S McBride; 23 AA/S McBride; 24 AA/C Sawyer; 24/25 AA/C Sawyer; 26/27 AA/S McBride; 27tr AA/J Smith; 28 AA/S McBride; 29 AA/J Smith; 30 AA/S McBride; 31 AA/S McBride; 32 AA/S McBride; 33l AA/J Smith; 33r AA/J Smith; 34 AA/C Sawyer; 35 AA/S McBride; 36l AA/S McBride; 36r AA/C Sawyer; 37 AA/S McBride; 38t AA/J Wyand; 38b AA/S McBride; 39 AA/C Sawyer; 40cl AA/S McBride; 40bl AA/C Sawyer; 40bc AA/J Smith; 41bl AA/J Smith; 41br AA/C Sawyer; 42 AA/C Sawyer; 43 AA/C Sawyer; 44/45 AA/J Smith; 45 AA/J Smith; 46/47 AA/J Smith; 46bl AA/J Smith; 47r AA/J Smith; 48/49 AA/S McBride; 49r AA/S McBride; 50l AA/S McBride; 50r AA/S McBride; 51 AA/S McBride; 52/53 AA/S McBride; 53r AA/S McBride; 54/55 AA/J Smith; 56 AA/S McBride; 57 AA/C Sawyer; 58 AA/J Wyand; 58/59 AA/C Sawyer; 59r AA/J Wyand; 60 AA/J Smith; 61 AA/J Smith; 62/63 AA/S McBride; 64t AA/S McBride; 64b AA/J Smith; 65l AA/S McBride; 65r AA/S McBride; 66 AA/J Wyand; 67 AA/J Wyand; 68 AA/J Smith; 69 AA/J Smith; 70 AA/J Smith; 71l AA/J Smith; 71r AA/J Smith; 72 AA/S McBride; 73 AA/S McBride; 74 AA/J Smith; 75 AA/J Smith; 76cl AA/J Smith; 76bl AA/J Wyand; 76br Jan Kruml; 77bl AA/J Wyand; 77br AA/J Smith; 78 AA/J Smith; 79 AA/J Smith; 80 AA/J Smith; 81t AA/T Souter; 81b AA/J Smith; 82 AA/S McBride 83 AA/S McBride; 84 AA/S McBride; 85 AA/J Smith/Jewish Museum Prague; 86 AA/S McBride; 87 AA/S McBride; 88 AA/J Smith; 89 AA/J Smith/Jewish Museum Prague; 90/91 AA/J Wyand; 91 AA/T Souter; 92 AA/J Wyand; 93 AA/C Sawyer; 94 AA/T Souter; 95 AA/J Wyand; 96 AA/C Sawyer; 97t AA/J Wyand; 97b AA/S McBride; 98/99 AA/J Smith; 99tr AA/J Smith; 100 Jan Kruml; 102 AA/C Sawyer; 103 AA/S McBride; 104t AA/S McBride; 104b AA/S McBride; 105 AA/T Souter; 106cl AA/S McBride; 106bl AA/C Sawyer; 106br AA/J Smith; 107bl AA/S McBride; 107br AA/S McBride; 108 AA/S McBride; 109 AA/S McBride; 110 AA/S McBride; 111 AA/T Souter; 112/113 AA/S McBride; 113 AA/S McBride; 114 AA/S McBride; 115l AA/S McBride; 115r AA/S McBride; 116 AA/J Smith; 117 AA/J Smith; 118 AA/J Wyand; 120 AA/J Smith; 121l AA/J Smith; 121r AA/J Smith; 122/123 AA/C Sawyer; 123 AA/J Wyand; 124t AA/C Sawyer; 124b AA/S McBride; 125 AA/J Smith; 126cl AA/J Smith; 126bl AA/J Smith; 126bc AA/J Smith; 127br AA/S McBride; 127bc AA/S McBride; 128 AA/J Smith; 129 Profimedia International s.r.o./Alamy; 130/131 AA/S McBride; 131 AA/J Smith © Mucha Trust 2007/The Bridgeman Art Library; 132/133 AA/J Smith; 133 AA/S McBride; 134 AA/J Smith; 135 AA/J Wyand; 136/137 AA/J Wyand; 137 AA/J Smith; 138 AA/S McBride; 139 AA/J Smith; 140 AA/S McBride; 141 AA/S McBride; 142 AA/J Wyand; 143 AA/J Wyand; 144t AA/S McBride; 144b AA/J Smith; 145 AA/J Smith; 146 AA/T Souter; 147 AA/C Sawyer; 148 AA/J Wyand; 149 AA/J Wyand; 150 AA/J Smith; 150/151 AA/J Smith; 152 AA/J Smith; 153 AA/S McBride; 154 AA/J Smith; 155 AA/ C Sawyer; 158 AA/J Smith; 159 AA/S McBride; 160 AA/S McBride; 166 AA/J Smith; 172 AA/J Smith; 177 AA/J Smith; 178 AA/J Wyand; 182 AA/J Wyand; 183 AA/J Smith; 185 AA/J Smith; 188 AA/J Smith

Every effort has been made to trace the copyright holders, and we apologise in advance for any accidental errors. We would be happy to apply the corrections in the following edition of this publication.

The Automobile Association would like to thank all other contributors to this publication.

Notes

Notes